Principles
& Concepts

Tai Chi Chuan Revelations

TAI CHI CHUAN REVELATIONS

Principles and Concepts

by
Grandmaster Ip Tai Tak
5th Generation
Yang Family Tai Chi Chuan

Translated by
Master Ding Teah Chean

Tai Chi Chuan Revelations:
Principles & Concepts

© *Copyright 2001 by Ding Teah Chean*

First Edition

First published in 2001 by
**Tai Chi Worldwide Limited,
P.O Box 6404,
London E18 1EX,
United Kingdom.**

Tel: 020 8502 9307 Fax: 020 8551 7553
*Email : tcah@taichiwl.demon.co.uk
website : www.taichiwl.demon.co.uk*

Cover designed by Vardeep Gahir

Printed in United Kingdom by Bell & Bain Ltd, Glasgow

ISBN 0-9541155-0-3
A catalogue record of this book is available from the British Library.

Caution:

The descriptions and instructions in this book are no substitute for an experienced and qualified teacher. Any application of the principles and concepts in this book is at the reader's sole discretion and risk.

Dedication

This book is
dedicated to my master,
Great Grandmaster Yang Sau Chung,
4th Generation Head of the
Yang Family Tai Chi Chuan, and
to all Tai Chi Chuan practitioners
seeking a better understanding
and insight into the
Traditional Yang Family
Tai Chi Chuan.

Grandmaster Ip Tai Tak

Grandmaster Ip Tai Tak

5th Generation Yang Family Tai Chi Chuan

One of the world's leading authorities on the Traditional Yang Family Tai Chi Chuan

Grandmaster Ip Tai Tak, as a keen young martial artist, first encountered Great Grandmaster Yang Sau Chung in 1951 when the latter gave a public demonstration exhibiting the Traditional Yang Family Tai Chi Chuan.

After four years of dedicated study, he was accepted as the first disciple of Great Grandmaster Yang and continued his study until his teacher passed away in 1985. Now at 72 years, Grandmaster Ip is still as devoted as ever to the study, practice and development of the Traditional Yang Family Tai Chi Chuan, teaching a small number of senior students.

He is "open" in his teaching and willing to share his knowledge of Tai Chi Chuan with those of the right attitude and commitment to pursuing the art to the highest level.

Contents

Preface		*14*
Acknowledgements		*20*
Translator's Note		*22*
Yang Family Tai Chi Chuan Lineage		*24*

Chapter

1.	Wang Tsung Yueh's Thirteen Postures of Chi Circulatory Movements	42
2	Hang Kung Kou Jue	58
3	Wang Chung Yueh's Tai Chi Quan Lun	66
4	Chen Wei Ming's Tai Chi Quan Lun	80
5	Da Shou Ge (The Song of Push Hands)	82
6	Yang Cheng Fu's Ten Principles of Tai Chi Chuan	88
7	Explanation of the Essence of the Five Elements	96
8	Explanation of the Slow Movement Without Physical Strength in Tai Chi Chuan	102
9	Thirteen Essential Points of Tai Chi Chuan	106
10	Twelve Illnesses in Tai Chi Chuan	110
11	Twelve Essential Elements of Tai Chi Chuan	114
12	Extract from Wudang Gong Fu Series	118
13	Tai Chi Chuan Posture Checking	126
14	Yang Family Old Manual	132
15	Tai Chi Chuan Terminology	144
16	Conclusion	162

Appendix:

1.	*Grandmaster Ip's TCAH Interview*	*166*
2.	*Traditional Yang Family Tai Chi Chuan Form*	*176*
3.	*Traditional Yang Family Sword Form*	*184*
4.	*Traditional Yang Style Sabre Form*	*188*
5.	*Traditional Thirteen Spear Techniques*	*192*
6.	*Glossary*	*196*
7.	*Miscellaneous*	*200*
8.	*Notes*	*208*

Preface
by
Master Ding Teah Chean
(also known as John Ding)

Tai Chi Chuan has many labels. Some identify it as a martial art, whilst others view it as a spiritual discipline or health exercise. However, none of these labels can claim to categorise the 'art' exclusively. Tai Chi Chuan fails to fall neatly into one classification. Hence it gathers numerous descriptions and thus interpretations - some good, some bad and some indifferent, and Tai Chi Chuan's true definition remains elusive to many.

However, most enthusiasts would argue that Tai Chi Chuan is a discipline. It is a discipline that binds together the physical, the mental and the spiritual. Only when these three essential human qualities are embraced and united can a pure new entity be formed. It is this we call *The Great Ultimate,* or *Tai Chi.* In fact, together the three Chinese words *Tai Chi Chuan* literally translate as *The Great Ultimate Fist.* Perhaps this more bare approach may help in some way to elucidate Tai Chi Chuan's true essence.

This is not a book that offers The Great Ultimate. That is a goal which can only be achieved by the individual. Instead, the aim of this book is to empower the Tai Chi Chuan practitioner with the opportunity to grow and mature at many levels. It provides fundamental elements needed for development, and gives direction to one's journey along a path well travelled by ambassadors of Tai Chi Chuan. Tai Chi Revelations should be used as a tool to exercise the mind, as well as feed the spirit. However, its intention is not to substitute the practical but rather to encourage and enhance it by nurturing the theoretical.

Tai Chi Revelations is a book which took two years to translate but almost fifty years to research and compose. It is directly translated from a chronological logbook that has been kept up to date for almost half a century. These handwritten records are the representation of one man's single-minded pursuit of excellence, a man who is an extraordinary scholar of Tai Chi Chuan. This man is my mentor and *Sifu*, Grandmaster Ip Tai Tak.

Grandmaster Ip Tai Tak - fifth generation of Yang family Tai Chi Chuan and first disciple of Great Grandmaster Yang Sau Chung - is one of the few remaining forefront figures in Yang Style Tai Chi Chuan today. Grandmaster Ip has vast experience and understanding with knowledge that spans a lifetime of disciplined and devoted practice. He has a reputation that precedes him and a title that demands attention from genuine Tai Chi practitioners.

To this day Grandmaster Ip still maintains entries in his memoirs. Diligent and methodical, he remains faithful to the study, practice and development of Tai Chi Chuan. His lifetime achievements have brought him recognition worldwide. However, he is a man who takes little interest in fame. He is a humble individual whose face carries the mark of experience, and whose expressions tell a hundred stories, yet to the uninitiated he relies little on the spoken word. Preferring a life away from the public eye, Grandmaster Ip, like those in the tradition before him, continues to explore and thus to expand the boundaries of Tai Chi Chuan.

The concept of responsibility is central to the tradition of lineage: responsibility not only to further the development of Tai Chi Chuan by pushing back the known limits of the art, but also to preserve the complete art and its transmissions. Lineage holders must have the ability to receive true transmission from their masters, and ensure that this transmission is passed on appropriately to the next generation. The rare act of discipleship or *Bai Shi* signifies transmission passing from master to disciple, from one generation to another. It describes a complex bond that has formed between master and chosen disciple. A tie that involves more than just the preservation of subject matter, discipleship represents a relationship that is deeply personal, where the master, his disciple and the bond between them hold central significance.

On the 1st January 1998, I was privileged to become part of this traditional relationship by being accepted as the first disciple of Grandmaster Ip Tai Tak. Just as Grandmaster Ip took responsibility as a primary lineage holder in 1955 by accepting his role as the first disciple of Great Grandmaster Yang Sau Chung, I take the same responsibility, with the acceptance of my role as Grandmaster Ip's first disciple. However, years on from my discipleship, the importance of representing the sixth generation of Yang Family Tai Chi Chuan is secondary to the relationship I have formed with my Master. This bond is indescribable with the written word. It encompasses trust, humility, honesty, and mutual respect, and goes beyond duty, dedication, and admiration.

I am perpetually guided by Grandmaster Ip's unique depth of understanding and his inexhaustible experience. Two points on the same line to a common goal, we not only continue to *Gau Sau* (exchange hands), but also constantly share our thoughts, ideas, and expectations, using his logbooks as a frame of reference. These logbooks are the written record of Grandmaster Ip's daily thoughts and perceptions of Yang Family Tai Chi Chuan. Diaries that reach back fifty years into history, they follow the intimate thirty year master-disciple relationship between Great Grandmaster Yang Sau Chung and Grandmaster Ip Tai Tak. They record in detail the daily transmissions from Great Grandmaster Yang Sau Chung, and contain meticulously drawn diagrams, which serve to clarify many Tai Chi principles. With a wealth of rare knowledge, Grandmaster Ip's handwritten Chinese scripts contain both the subjective and the objective, the former by clearly laying out his own and other people's thoughts and concepts, and the latter by providing historical documentation of events and politics of the era.

The publication of Grandmaster Ip's memoirs was certainly never planned. However, with an increasing awareness of the responsibility to promote and disseminate the true teachings of Tai Chi Chuan, both Grandmaster Ip and myself understood the growing importance of his memoirs. Our publication would at last offer authentic representation of Tai Chi Chuan from an authoritative source, as well as provide some insight into the world behind the closed doors of Yang Family Tai Chi Chuan.

It was with Grandmaster Ip's permission and blessing that I began to make preparations for the publication of his memoirs. From early on it was clear that with the vast wealth of information contained within these logbooks, it would not have been possible to publish the diaries in one complete volume. Instead, to do the diaries justice, publication required several volumes. So in 1998, work began with the aid of my students. We meticulously dissected the memoirs, grouping the texts held within into defined themes. This would thus prioritise subject matter above chronology, and hence provide the Tai Chi practitioner with a powerful source of reference that would be comprehensive and easily accessible.

Then came the mammoth task of translating Grandmaster Ip's handwritten Chinese scripts into clear, straightforward English. My first care was to make certain the meaning of the passages within the memoirs by maintaining close interaction with the author, Grandmaster Ip, throughout the translation process. The next was to ensure the translation remained faithful to the original, as well as intelligible to both beginners and advanced practitioners of Tai Chi Chuan. This turned out to be a complex task. With a core group working together, this first volume of Tai Chi Chuan Revelations underwent numerous drafts, taking more than two years to complete.

This first volume of Tai Chi Chuan Revelations focuses on Tai Chi Chuan principles and concepts. Grandmaster Ip shares his insight and deep understanding of Tai Chi Chuan and explains original concepts not found elsewhere. He also stresses the importance of other Tai Chi Chuan authors and texts, and takes a bold step by revealing the unspoken interpretation of many old Tai Chi Chuan scripts. Interleaved between the English, Tai Chi Revelations also contains passages of Chinese characters directly transcribed from Grandmaster Ip's logbook as well as including rare photographs taken from Grandmaster Ip's personal album.

I hope Tai Chi Chuan Revelations will provide the reader with all the wealth of insight and understanding they have given me. This book has been a personal achievement not only for me but for all those involved with its production. Without all the hard work from the entire team it would not have become a reality. However, let us not forget that without one man's selfless dedication to the discipline of Tai Chi Chuan, this book would have been an impossibility and the art would not be as rich as it is today. Grandmaster Ip Tai Tak, my *Sifu*, is truly an ambassador of Tai Chi Chuan.

I leave you with this final thought, courtesy of Grandmaster Ip:

But Da But Gau:

Not to hit is not to teach *

---

* *Whilst texts serve to aid understanding, an exchange of hands will always provide a clarity of understanding that surpasses words.*

Acknowledgements

I would like to specially express my thanks and gratitude to my first disciple, Ding Teah Chean (or John Ding). He has been able to successfully transcribe and translate my diaries, with the aid of his students, into a succinct and comprehensive book. **Tai Chi Chuan Revelations - Principles and Concepts** is a book that I am pleased to call my own; however, it has taken John Ding's team over two years to complete, and we have them to thank for this piece of work.

At this book's heart is the aim to present the Tai Chi Chuan principles and concepts from my memoirs in an organised fashion. Just to separate these accounts from the rest of my memoirs was a huge task in itself; but in addition to this, to translate them with such consideration that they remain faithful to the original is an undertaking I do not look upon lightly. It took commitment, dedication, and strength to be able to achieve this goal, and judging from the results it seems that the whole team have these characteristics in abundance. Thus I would like to personally thank the following students of my disciple, John Ding:

Dr. Alan Ding - for his analytical manner in assisting with the translation and the proof reading of the original manuscript.

Mak Wah Hoi - a pivotal member of the team who worked closely with John Ding throughout the whole project. For tirelessly providing translations from the memoirs, transcribing Chinese passages of text and proof-reading manuscripts.

Philippa Kennedy - for proof-reading draft upon draft, offering numerous suggestions to improve the content of the book, and providing a sense of calm to the whole team.

Doosyant Mahadeo – for proof reading and adding constructive ideas for this book.

Vardeep Gahir - for designing the cover of this publication.

and lastly to all of his students who have assisted in the proofing of the manuscript and providing valuable suggestions for the publication of this book.

Translator's Note

We have tried to keep the English translation as near to the original Chinese (using the Chinese *Pu Tong Hua Pinyin* romanisation of Chinese to English) as possible. However, as is well known, there are great differences between the two languages. Chinese characters are pictorial representations of concepts, and are often very complex, ambiguous and poetic, in contrast to the English alphabetic writing system. This means that a completely literal translation would not make enough sense to serve the purpose of this book – i.e. to provide a clear and practical manual of instruction in the art of Tai Chi Chuan to English speakers. We have therefore tried to aim for a direct and simple style of English, in order to provide a type of 'bridge' between the two languages, rather than a slavish translation.

However, the translations of the old Chinese phrases quoted by Grandmaster Ip have been kept very close to the original in order to convey their picturesque 'flavour' (for example: *'Cannot add the weight of a feather. A fly not able to alight. Others do not know me, but I alone know others. One becomes invincible when one masters all these principles'* – from *The Old Classic Manual*). These phrases are then interpreted and clarified by Master Ip. The original Chinese ideograms have been used together with these phrases, to further ensure that the meaning is not lost. They have also been included for people who wish to take their study of Tai Chi Chuan further by learning Chinese writing. Every layer of language leads to a different, deeper perception and understanding.

Although the different sections of this volume form an organic whole, each chapter may also be read as an individual unit, and can thus stand on its own. In this way, the book can be repeatedly referred to and conveniently dipped into again and again, to get new and different insights, both for beginners and more advanced students.

Finally, the Glossary at the end explains the common Chinese terms used throughout this book for easy reference.

The Yang Family Tai Chi Chuan Lineage

of Grandmaster Ip

Yang Family Lineage

Statue of **Chen Chang Hsing**, Yang Lu Chan's master

Yang Family Lineage

Yang Lu Chan, Founder of the Yang Family Tai Chi Chuan

Yang Chien Hou, 2nd Generation, Youngest Son of Yang Lu Chan

Yang Family Lineage

Yang Cheng Fu, 3rd Generation, Youngest Son of Yang Chien Hou

Yang Family Lineage

Yang Sau Chung, 4th Generation, Eldest Son of Yang Cheng Fu

Yang Family Lineage

Ip Tai Tak, 5th Generation, First Disciple of Yang Sau Chung

Ding Teah Chean, 6th Generation, First Disciple of Ip Tai Tak

Yang Family Lineage

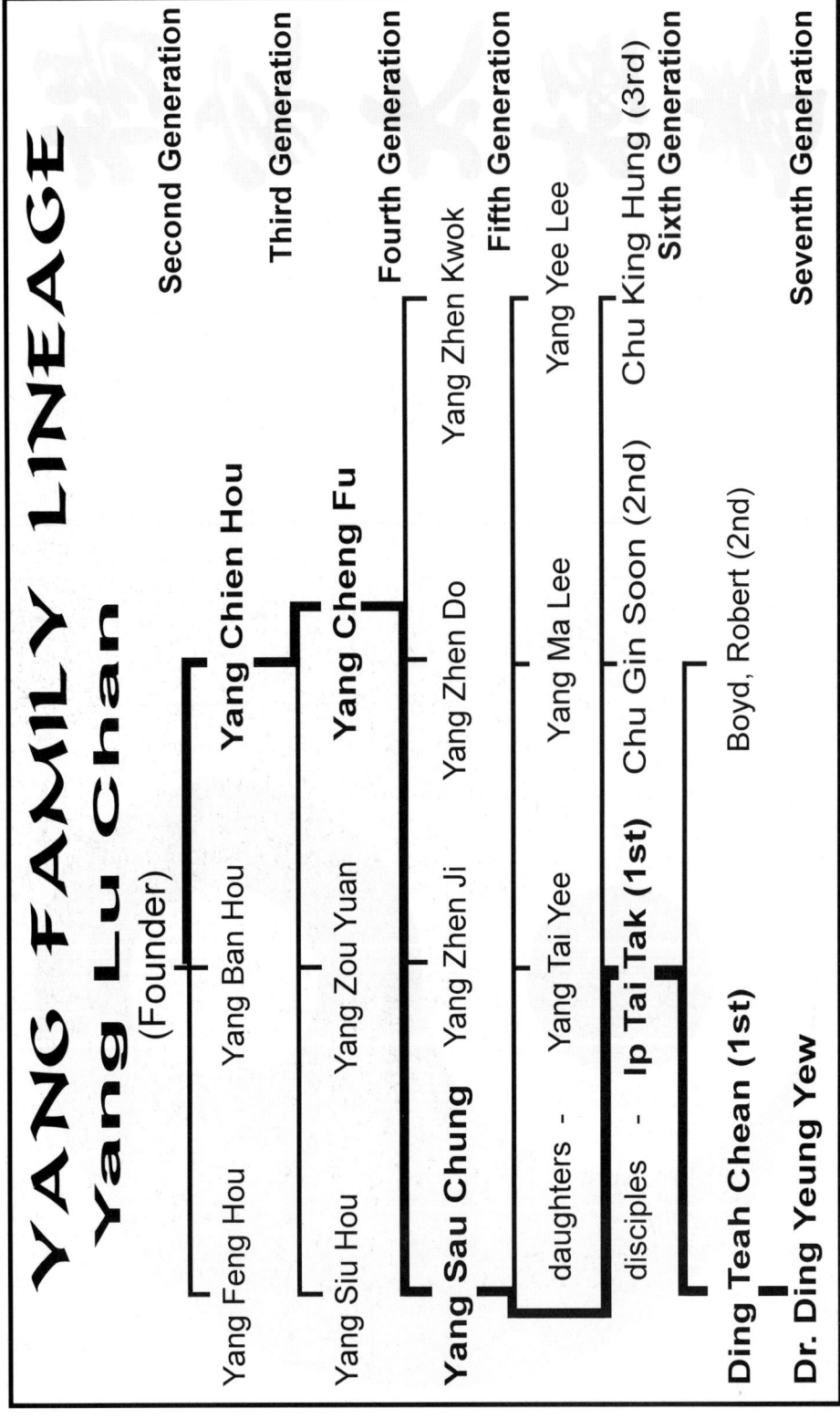

Yang Family Lineage

Grandmaster Ip and his first disciple, Master Ding

Master Ding Teah Chean (or John Ding)

6th Generation, Yang Family Tai Chi Chuan

John Ding, BA (Hons), DMS, began his study of martial arts at an early age, under various Shaolin Kung Fu masters before devoting himself entirely to the internal system of Tai Chi Chuan. He is one of the few people to have studied under all three formal disciples of the late Grandmaster Yang Sau Chang.

On the first of January 1998, John Ding, founder of the John Ding International Academy of Tai Chi Chuan based in London, was accepted as the first disciple of Master Ip Tai Tak.

John Ding is the 6th Generation of the Yang Family Tai Chi Chuan lineage through Grandmaster Ip Tai Tak.

Yang Family Lineage

Dr. Ding Yeung Yew (or Alan Ding)

7th Generation, Yang Family Tai Chi Chuan

Dr. Alan Ding, MBBS began his study of Tai Chi Chuan at the early age of five under his father, Master Ding. During his Tai Chi Chuan training, he has also studied under Master Chu Gin Soon (2nd Disciple of Great Grandmaster Yang Sau Chung), who teaches in Boston, USA.

In his pursuit of excellence in Yang Family Tai Chi Chuan, he still continues his studies with his father and Grandmaster Ip.

He is a doctor in one of the United Kingdom's National Health Service hospitals, as well as being an accomplished Yang Family Tai Chi Chuan practitioner and Chief Instructor of the John Ding International Academy of Tai Chi Chuan based in London.

Dr. Alan Ding is the 7th Generation of the Yang Family Tai Chi Chuan lineage through Grandmaster Ip Tai Tak.

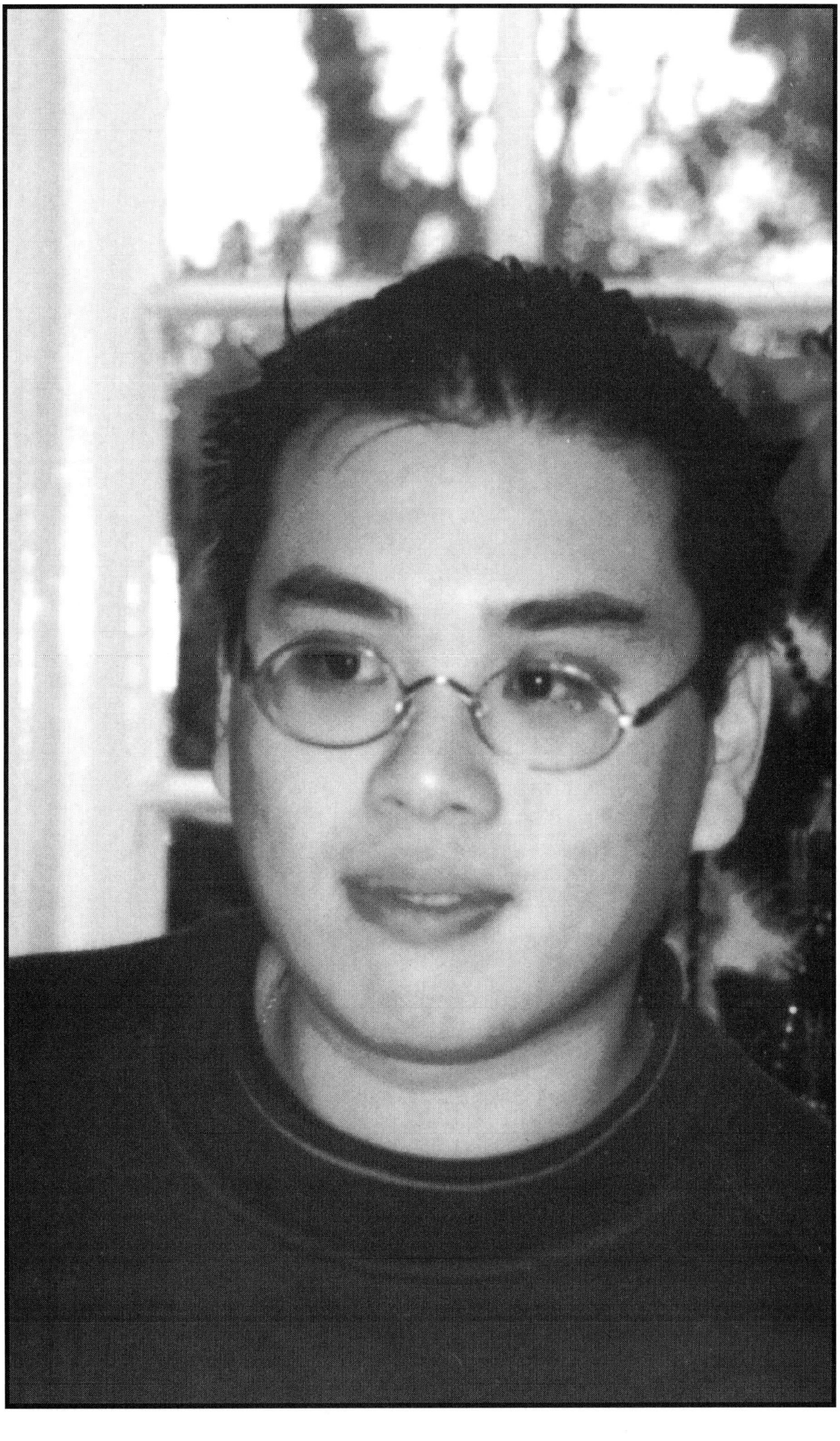

1965 Anniversary of Great Grandmaster Yang Sau Chung's Tai Chi Chuan School

Great Grandmaster Yang San Chung and Grandmaster Ip, demonstrating the application of weapons at the Anniversary

Grandmaster Ip's first visit to London in 1999 to attend the Yang 200 Celebration Event of Yang Lu Chan, organised by Master Ding. Picture of all participants in the show.

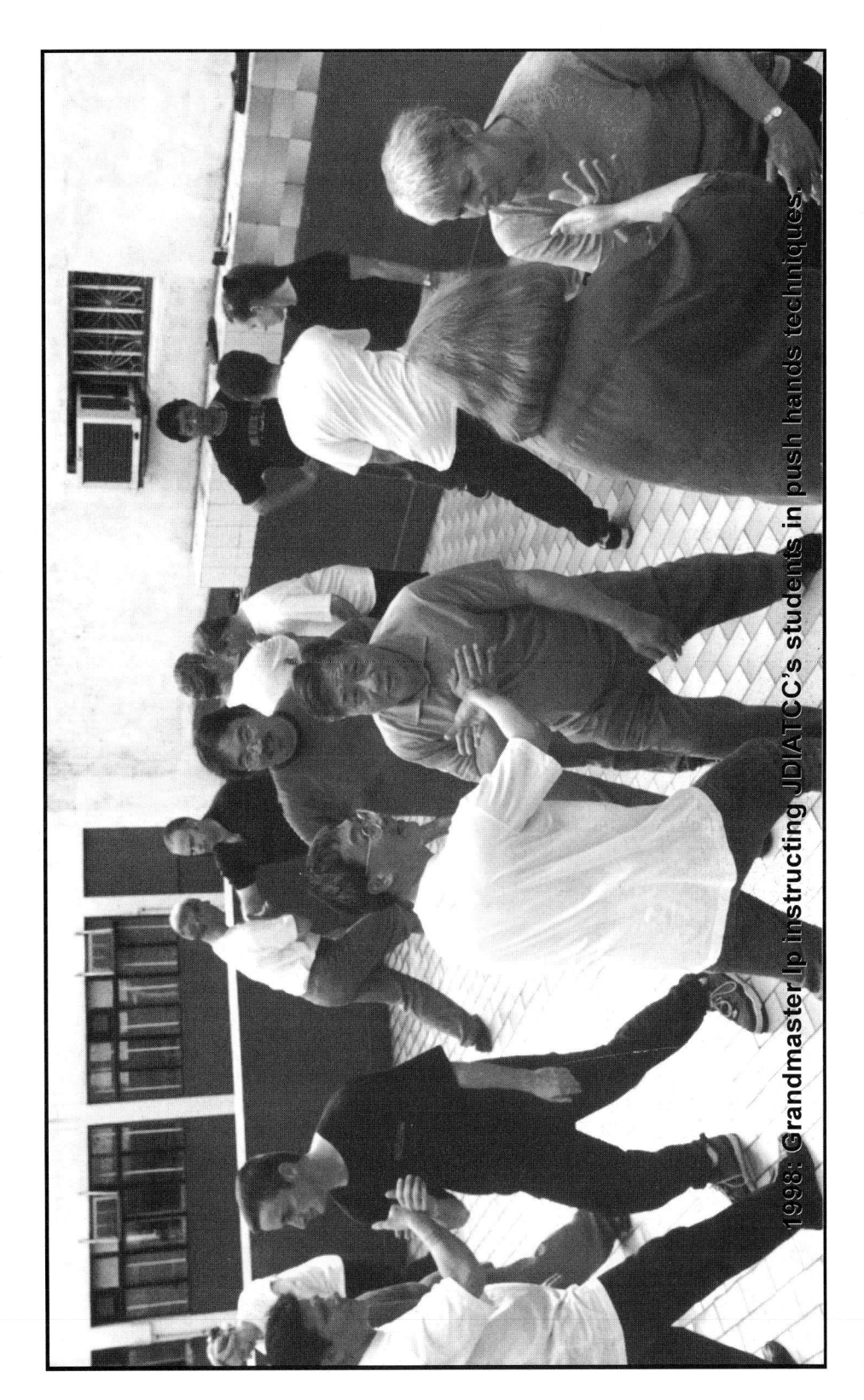

1998: Grandmaster Ip instructing JDIATCC's students in push hands techniques.

Chapter 1

十三勢行功心解

Wang Tsung Yueh's
Thirteen Postures of Chi Circulatory Movements

以心行氣，務令沉著，乃能收斂入骨。

Translation:
Use the "Xin" (or "heart") to circulate the Chi to ensure that it sinks, and thus enable it to gather in the bones.

Explanation:
The Chinese character for *"Xin"* (i.e. 心) in this context refers to the intent of the mind. To enable the *Chi* to circulate, one must use the intent of the mind to move the *Chi*, hence the phrase:

意到氣到   *"Yi Dou Chi Dou"*

Chinese or translated meaning :
When the intent arrives, Chi energy will also arrive

The intention should focus on sinking and settling the *Chi* to enable it to gather in the bones. This process will enhance *Chi* circulation around the body. With the intention of sinking, the breathing becomes natural and effortless. Such gathering of *Chi* in the bones over time makes the bones grow stronger and heavier and results in the growth of one's internal power.

以氣運身，務令順遂，乃能便利從心。

Translation:
Circulate the Chi in the body through gentle and continuous movement. The Xin (or heart) will direct the flow with ease.

Explanation:
To circulate the *Chi* in the body means that for the *Chi* to move,

there must be appropriate body movements. The flow of *Chi* must be without obstruction. This results in the natural internal movements of *Chi* as directed by *Yi* (or intention of the mind). Therefore any changes in movements are easily carried out through one's wishes, without any hindrance.

This also means that when practising the Tai Chi Chuan form, one must ensure that the thirteen basic postures conform to the principles and concepts of Tai Chi Chuan. This will ensure more concentrated circulation of *Chi*.

精神能提得起，則無遲重之虞，所謂頭頂懸也。

Translation:
With ability to raise the spirit, there will be no presence of sluggishness. This is sometimes referred to as :

頭頂懸　**Tou Ding Xuan**
or to suspend one's head.

Explanation:
"*Tou Ding Xuan*" means one should straighten the back of the neck, as if suspended on a string and also push the head upwards as if against the ceiling at the same time. A clear passage results, which enables the free flow of *Chi* upwards. This leads to a feeling of being more alert and refreshed. Consequently, the body is light, flexible and nimble. We can thus easily distinguish the difference between using the mind and physical strength. Any movement relying on physical strength is more rigid and less easy to redirect.

意氣須換得靈，乃有圓活之妙，
所謂變轉虛實也。

Translation:
The interchange between intent and Chi must be expeditious and agile. It creates a feeling of wholeness and liveliness. This is what the interplay between

虛　***Xu*** *(or insubstantial) and*

實　***Shi*** *(or substantial) is all about.*

Explanation:
When sticking to the opponent, one must be able to change one's intention in response to any change in the opponent's reactions. This involves a clear understanding of the concept of *Xu* (insubstantial) and *Shi* (substantial). Hence, the essence of wholeness and liveliness can be fully experienced.

發勁須沉著鬆淨，專注一方。

Translation:
To project Jin (勁) or essence of the power, one needs to be calm, relaxed and focused towards one direction with concentration.

Explanation:
When releasing *Jin,* the whole body should be relaxed and without any distraction to the mind. If one is not relaxed, one cannot sink and bring forth the power. On the other hand, when one sinks and is focused, the *Jin* projected is even more intense and powerful. To concentrate in one direction means to follow the opponent's

direction of movements and direct the power straight to it. The direction of attack is guided by the direction of sight with intention. For example, when throwing the opponent upwards, your eyes and intention should be directed upwards; to throw your opponent downwards, you look downwards or to throw your opponent further away, you look and project beyond. When the *Shen* (or spirit) is present, *Chi* is present and no physical strength is necessary.

立身須中正安舒，撐支八面。

Translation:
Postures must be straight and erect, centred, tranquil and extended so that one is rooted and able to project in all eight directions.

Explanation:
"*Tou Ding Xuan*" i.e. when one suspends the head, one will automatically stand straight, erect and centred. When relaxed and calm, one will be tranquil and able to extend. One then becomes rooted and remains stable like a mountain. If one is calm and settled internally, one will be able to anticipate through stillness. The waist acts as an axle while the hand and shoulder act as the wheel. This rotation allows one to deal with attacks from all directions.

行氣如九曲珠，無微不到。

Translation:
Circulating the Chi like " threading nine crooked pearls", reaching every extremity.

Explanation:
The body is like a string of pearls containing "crooked" channels (i.e. neck, chest, shoulder, elbow, wrist, hip, coccyx, knee, & ankle) where the *Chi* needs to flow through bends and corners. When all these pearls are linked together via the flow of unbroken *Chi,* then one achieves the unison of mind and *Chi.* This demonstrates the number of obstructions one has to encounter and the painstaking practice one has to go through to get all these pearls linked together.

運勁如百煉鋼，何堅不摧。

Translation:
To circulate Jin power like tempering steel hundreds of times, making it able to destroy any known hardness.

Explanation:
Internal power requires time and effort to attain. It cannot be achieved overnight. It compares to wrought iron before it is turned into steel, as it requires tempering hundreds of times to turn it into good quality steel. The acquiring of such power through regular practice of Tai Chi Chuan would enable one to destroy even the hardest of objects. If the opponent is just flesh and blood, he will not be able to stand against such potent force. In essence, Tai Chi Chuan does not rely on physical strength but uses the developed

internal power, *Chi*. Such power is limitless!

形如搏兔之鷹，神如捕鼠之貓。

Translation:
The body is like the eagle preying on the rabbit. The spirit is like the cat about to pounce on the mouse.

Explanation:
Like the eagle that continually circles in the sky when preying on the rabbit, one's position is never static. Like the crouching cat about to pounce, one waits in stillness for the opportunity to strike. Whether in movement or in stillness, the intention is always present.

靜如山岳，動若江河。

Translation:
Still like a mountain. Move like a roaring river.

Explanation:
Still like a mountain means sinking solidly without floating. When one practises for a long time, it is like growing roots under the feet. Hence, one is not easily moved or shaken by human strength. Move like a roaring river means continuous flow without end. This symbolises endless changes that can be derived from one movement into ten, ten to hundreds and hundreds to thousands and so on.

蓄勁如張弓，發勁如放箭。

Translation:
Storing the power is like a drawn bow. Releasing the power is like shooting an arrow.

Explanation:
Tai Chi Chuan power is hidden within and cannot be seen externally. The internal power is stored as in a drawn bow or in a fully inflated balloon. As soon as the opponent presses down on your shoulder, he cannot push down even though he feels the softness of your body. You are like a bow. As soon as the opponent makes contact, he will be thrown out like an arrow being shot. The opponent will not even be aware of the throw until he has landed. This emphasises the fullness and speed of the execution of internal power.

曲中求直，蓄然後發。

Translation:
From within the curve search for straightness. Store before issuing.

Explanation:
The curve will neutralise the opponent's strength. Once his power is neutralized you can search for the straight line into your opponent, enabling you to project your internal power. It takes much practice and experience in order to find this straight line.

力由脊發，步隨身換．

Translation:
Chi power is issued from the back. Footwork follows changes in posture.

Explanation:
Hollow the chest to raise the back in order to gather and focus the *Chi* for application. When projecting the power, the power should come through the hands from the back, and not from the physical strength of the arms. When the body moves, the feet follow so that any changes are undefined.

收即是放，放即是收，斷而復連．

Translation:
To draw is to release. To release is to draw. Any breakages will be rejoined.

Explanation:
To stick, to neutralise and to attack are three different intentions which cannot be separated. To draw is to stick and neutralise. To release is to attack. When releasing, although the power may appear to be broken, the three intentions of sticking, neutralising and attacking still persist.

往復須有摺叠，進退須有轉換。

Translation:
To and fro movements must have a folding action. Advance and retreat movements are interchangeable.

Explanation:
To and fro movements with repeated folding action allow continuous flow, thus enabling one to apply the concept of substantial and insubstantial. When applying substantial and insubstantial concepts, only very small, subtle action is required in the movement. Tai Chi Chuan *Jie Jin* (intercepting energy) often requires this folding action. In outward appearance, there is no movement, as the folding action has already taken place from within. Advance and retreat require changes of footwork. As you retreat you are also in reality advancing (a concept often misunderstood by practitioners!)

極柔軟然後極堅剛，能呼吸然後能靈活。

Translation:
Extreme softness will lead to extreme hardness. Breathing naturally will lead to greater agility and nimbleness.

Explanation:
Lao Tze said,

> "Extreme softness in the universe can overcome extreme hardness in the universe.
> So extreme softness is also extreme strength".

Breathing naturally refers to the heavenly way of breathing. To inhale is to lift and to absorb. To exhale is to sink and to release. This is the heavenly way of breathing and is opposite to normal breathing. It enables one to lift up and throw an opponent with ease. When the breathing is smooth and natural, movements are easier to perform and have greater flexibility.

氣以直養而無害，勁以曲蓄而有餘。

Translation:
No harm comes from nourishing the Chi. The "Jin" force is stored within the curvature and with excess to spare.

Explanation:
Mencius states that the heavenly *Chi* is the strongest and most powerful force in the universe. Nourishing the *Chi* will not cause any harm to the body as it lies between heaven and earth. Tai Chi Chuan is an ancient Chinese exercise system which focuses on *Chi* nourishment. With daily practice you develop internally without realising. Over time, you develop a sense of fullness from emptiness and become extremely strong and potent. When the *Chi* energy is required, it is already stored and ready for use. When applied, the power is "full" and cannot be defended against.

心為令，氣為旗，腰為纛。

Translation:
The Xin (heart) is the command, the Chi the "Qi"(旗 or flag) and the waist the "Dao" (纛 or banner).

Explanation:
The heart is the intention of the mind which directs the *Chi*, and hence the commander. In all situations, the waist acts as the banner to uphold the body structure and maintain balance.

先求開展，後求緊湊，乃可臻於縝密矣。

Translation:
First strive for a large and open structure, then for tightness, smoothness and continuous movement. You will ultimately reach an impenetrable state.

Explanation:
When practising the form or push hands, first start with a large and open circular structure. This trains the movement of the waist and legs. When you have acquired the skill, then strive for smaller and closer circular movements. Hence, go from a large to a small circle, and end with no circle. Often in push hands you will observe an advanced person able to uproot and unbalance an opponent with very small circular and almost imperceptible movements.

又曰，先在心，後在身，腹鬆淨，氣斂入骨，神舒體靜，刻刻在心。

Translation:
It is stated that all begins from the heart, followed by the body, with the abdomen relaxed and soft. Gather the Chi into the bones. The spirit remains relaxed, with the body in a calm and tranquil state. This must be borne in mind at all times.

Explanation:
Tai Chi Chuan is based on the mind and intention. The body comes last. There is a saying that the mind and the *Chi* are the master and the bones and flesh are the servants. The abdomen must be relaxed without any tension. Only then can the *Chi* easily permeate the bones. The spirit must be without stress and the body in a quiet still state. Thus, you can manage different situations with confidence, without getting into a state of anxiety or panic.

切記一動無有不動，一靜無有不靜

Translation:
Remember when you move, everything moves as well. When you are still, everything remains still.

Explanation:
In order for the above principle to work, both the external and internal movements must work at the same time, like *Yin-Yang*. The upper torso and the lower body must be co-ordinated.

牽動往來氣貼背，斂入脊骨，內固精神，外示安逸。

Translation:
In any movement to and fro, the Chi is always at the back and will permeate the spine. This enables one to sustain alertness internally, while externally remaining calm and relaxed.

Explanation:
In combat, when moving forward and backward, you should always keep the chest hollow to enable the back to rise. If the *Chi* is gathered and stored in the back, this allows it to permeate the spine. At this stage, you then wait for an opportunity to release the power. This explains the principle of releasing the power from the back. Otherwise, the strength only comes from the arms and legs. When you remain alert internally and calm externally, the mind is more focused and stable, instead of being in disarray.

邁步如貓行，運勁如抽絲。

Translation:
Move like a cat. When generating Jin power, it is like drawing a thread of silk from a cocoon.

Explanation:
The cat's movements are soft, gentle and fluid so it remains calm, composed and in control.

Drawing silk means a continuous, steady unbroken flow which seeks an opportunity to respond appropriately when needed.

全身意在精神不在氣，在氣則滯，有氣者無力，無氣者純剛。

Translation:
The mind should be focused on the whole body through the spirit and not on the "breathing" i.e. normal breathing. Relying on "breathing" is sluggish. If you hold the breath, you have no power. If the force is used without relying on intrinsic energy, it becomes hard physical strength.

Explanation:
Tai Chi Chuan relies purely on the mind, and does not focus on the breathing. Breathing here refers to the physical function acquired after birth. Real breathing, however, refers to the heavenly *Chi* acquired before birth. There is a limit to one's physical strength, but the power of the heavenly *Chi* is unlimited. A common example is that of a new-born baby who is able to lift itself up when holding on tight to your finger, even though the physical muscles are still undeveloped. A few months later, the baby is unable to do this when it starts to rely on physical strength, as the muscles are not able to cope with its weight.

氣如車軸，腰似車輪。

Translation:
Chi is like the wheel of a cart. The waist is like the axle.

Explanation:
The phrases here refer to the principle of motion of external and internal movement. The waist initiates any external movements whilst the *Chi* circulates within the body like a rotating wheel. This also involves the application of the principles described above.

祖上積德
大器晚成
如日方中
急流勇退

Calligraphy written by Grandmaster Ip

Chapter 2

行功口訣

Hang Gong Kou Jue
Discussion
of the Mechanics
of Tai Chi Chuan

一舉動，週身俱要輕靈。

Translation:
For every move, the whole body should be co-ordinated, agile and light.

Explanation:
Without the use of physical strength, every move will be agile and light; as a consequence, each move will be firmly rooted.

尤須貫串。

Translation:
The movements need to be linked and continuous.

Explanation:
The movements should be in a continuous flow without break. Any break will give an advantage to the opponent.

氣宜鼓盪，神宜內斂。

Translation:
The breathing should be like "Gu Dang" (or a resonating drum). The spirit should be hidden.

Explanation:
Breathing like *Gu Dang* means there will be no gaps. Breathe naturally with a continuous sequence of raising and lowering movements on inhaling and exhaling breath. This assists in massaging the internal organs and in co-ordinating the external movements as well, so as to achieve unity of body and mind. Such

action ensures that no gaps occur in the system.

The spirit means the state of mind which, when hidden and controlled, will not give rise to panic or interruption of the thought process. The state of mind can be shown externally: for example, when one is excited, one looks elated and of high spirit. When one is down, one lowers the head and sighs a lot! It should be noted that any external exhibition of one's state of mind will make this state of mind known to your opponent. Hence, when practising Tai Chi Chuan, one should always keep the spirit hidden within to allow for more focused concentration without the slightest distraction.

無使有凸凹處，無使有斷續處．

Translation:
There should be no dents or protrusions, no breaks or reconnections anywhere.

Explanation:
"Dents, protrusions, breaks and reconnections" refer to incorrect alignment in the body. Their presence makes it easy for the opponent to gain the advantage and take control. They are a main cause of defeat.

其根在腳，主宰於腰，形放於手指，由腳而腿而腰，總須完整一氣，向前退後，乃能得機得執。

Translation:
The root is in the feet and is dictated by the waist. The form appears at the hands. From the feet to the thighs, the thighs to the waist, all should move in unison. Whether advancing or retreating, the opportunity and situation are within your realm.

Explanation:
According to *Chuang Tze*, the individual rests on the heels. In Tai Chi Chuan, when the breathing is deep and extended, the *Chi* can rise to the crown of the head and can also sink to the heels. Any changes in movement will affect rooting in the feet. All movements start from the feet to the thighs and thighs to the waist, finishing at the fingers and moving in unison.

In Tai Chi Chuan, to release the power through the fingers and propel the opponent away is not done through the use of physical strength. The power is initiated from the heels up through the legs, waist and to the hands. They are all interconnected and must come together naturally. Only then does the opportunity present itself for you to deliver the power.

有不得機得勢處，身便散亂，其病必於腰腿求之。

Translation:
Inability to seize the opportunity and situation. The whole structure is fragmented and in disarray. Such illness derives from the waist and legs.

Explanation:
Failure to seize the initiative is a direct result of using the hands without the waist and legs. The hands have to use more muscular power (physical strength) which in turn leads to imbalance of the upper and lower structure of the body. When one is unable to generate *Chi* power, one should pay particular attention to the movement of the waist and legs.

上下前後左右皆然，凡此皆是，不在外面，有前即有後，有左即有右。

Translation:
Whether moving upward or downward, forward or backward, left or right, all involve the use of intention, "Yi", and are not based on external movements. Where there is upward movement there is downward movement, similarly with forward movement there is also a backward movement and, lastly, with a left movement there is also a right movement.

Explanation:
When moving in any direction, one must move the waist and legs to enable one to execute the movements with ease. With the turning of the waist and legs, one also possesses the ability to understand

oneself, the opponent and the situation. Without such *Yi* the turning of waist and legs are just aimless external movements.

如意要向上，即寓下意，若將物掀起而加以挫之力，斯其根自斷，乃壞之速而無疑•

Translation:
If one's intention is in the upward direction, one has to store the intention of going down. Lifting an object by adding more strength in order to sever the "root", then the speed of destroying it is unquestionable.

Explanation:
This means that in combat, one's movements should be able to change in accordance with the circumstances in an unpredictable manner, making the opponent only able to deal with one thing at a time while losing sight of the others. Such distraction will cause the opponent to be disorientated, thus allowing one to take the initiative and gain advantage.

虛實宜分清楚，一處自有一處虛實，處處總有一處虛實，週身節節貫串，無令絲毫間斷耳•

Translation:
Xu (or insubstantial) and Shi (or substantial) must be clearly distinguished. Every point has its own substantial and insubstantial state. Together the Xu and Shi co-exist. Every part of the body is linked together to ensure there are no gaps in between.

Explanation:

In both practice and in combat, the concept of *Xu* (insubstantial) and *Shi* (substantial) must always be applied. This is decided by the intention of the opponent: when the opponent is substantial, one becomes insubstantial and vice versa. Through these variations, one is able to anticipate and control the situation.

Exploring the concept of linking the body together further, *"linking"* means every section of the joints has the ability to become both *Xu* and *Shi*. Therefore, even if such linking is disconnected at the joint that is being pulled or dragged, the centre or core structure remains unaffected. At the time of application, all these sections can be connected together and become interdependent, as a snake would strike back with its head if attacked by a crane on the tail or vice-versa. When attacked in the middle, both the head and tail strike back together. This is also described as being nimble and agile. Another example is: lifting a steel bar weighing 1000 pounds is straightforward and easy for a person who possesses the strength. However, to lift a 1000-pound steel chain will be more difficult and require more effort as the chain is linked together in small sections. Hence, each part of the body should be able to function both individually or in unison with the rest of the body.

長拳者，如長江大海，滔滔不絕也。

Translation:
Long Fist is like the Yangtse River or an ocean. It surges continuously without cessation.

Explanation:

The Long Fist refers to Tai Chi Chuan. When practising, the movements should be a continuous flow like the tremendous strength of the mighty roaring Yangtse river. (There is also another Long Fist Form called *"Chang Chuan"* which is different from Tai Chi Chuan but contains the same essence).

十三勢者，掤、攎、擠、按、採、裂、肘、靠，此八卦也，進步、退步、右顧、左盼、中定，此五行也．

Translation:

The thirteen postures are : Peng (ward off), Lu (roll back), Ji (press), An (push), Cai (pull down), Lie (split), Zhou (elbow) and Kao (shoulder) which form Ba Gua (or the eight triagrams), and forward, backward, gazing right, gazing left and central equilibrium which are the Wu Hang (or five elements).

Explanation:

Peng, Lu, Ji and *An* are referred to as *Kan Li Zhen Dui:* that is, the four sides of the square. *Cai, Lie, Zhou* and *Kao* are also referred to in Chinese as *Gan Kun Gen Xun*: that is, the four corners. All these together are known as *Ba Gua*

Forward, backward, looking right, gazing left and central equilibrium refer to metal, wood, water, fire and earth - the *Wu Hang* (or Five Elements).

All these directions make up the thirteen main postures contained in the Tai Chi Chuan form.

Chapter 3

王宗岳
太極拳論

Wang Tsung Yueh's
Tai Chi Quan Lun
The Old Classic Manual
of Tai Chi Chuan

太極者，無極而生，陰陽之母也。

Translation:
Tai Chi evolves from Wu Chi, the mother of Yin and Yang.

Explanation:
Stillness is Wu Chi. Motion is Tai Chi.
Tai means "grand". *Chi* means "beginning" or "ultimate". The first movement from *Wu Chi* creates *Yin* and *Yang*. *Tai Chi* is the harmony between *Yin* and *Yang*. In Tai Chi Chuan, the movements revolve round the concept of substantial and insubstantial, *Yin* and *Yang*, activity and inactivity.

動之則分，靜之則合。

Translation:
In activity it separates and in inactivity it comes together.

Explanation:
Yin and *Yang* are two opposite and yet complementary forces. One cannot exist without the other. When mind and intention are initiated, the energy, *Chi,* can be moved in any direction. When one is still, everything returns to the source, i.e. the *Dan Tian*, and this state of balance becomes *Wu Chi*: mind and spirit united. The whole body is said to be in a state of emptiness, which can be activated at any time in accordance with the intention of the mind.

無過不及，隨屈就伸。

Translation:
Never over-extend or under-reach. Follow the curve and yield to extension.

Explanation:
When one over-extends or under-reaches, one loses balance, thus making such movements ineffective. When making contact and sticking to the opponent, one should respond according to the opponent's movements. When the opponent attacks in a curve, one extends, and vice versa, so that one acts in close co-ordination, without losing, resisting, over-extending or under-reaching.

人剛我柔謂之走，我順人背謂之黏。

Translation:
When the opponent employs physical force, one should counter with softness. The Chinese word "Zou" means "to flee" but in this context it means "to divert while seeming to flee". When one is in an unhindered position and the opponent is in an awkward position there is "Nian" (or adherence).

Explanation:
In combat, when both people use physical strength to counteract each other, both are just resisting each other's advances. If one is hard and the other is soft, there will be no obstructions and this means "diverting while seeming to flee". Any attacking force is neutralised and rendered ineffective. When the opponent's force is neutralised, he loses the centre and ends up in a precarious position. From this position one can gain unhindered access to the

opponent's centre. *Nian* (to adhere) means not to let the opponent get away by placing him in a disadvantaged position where he is unable to deploy any strength even though he may have tremendous physical power. These are just some examples of Tai Chi Chuan self-defence techniques.

動急則急應，動緩則緩隨，雖變化萬端，而其理惟一貫．

Translation:
Respond to quickness with swiftness and follow slowness with an unhurried motion. Although there are numerous variations, the main principle remains unchanged.

Explanation:
The pace of all movements should follow the opponent rather than be initiated by oneself so that one can adhere to the opponent without losing contact. To achieve this, no physical strength should be exerted from the arms or else you will be taking the initiative and not be able to feel, adhere and follow the opponent. The movements can be in any direction and at different speeds, but the principles of "adhering" and "following" remain the same. If one can apply the principles, then one can react to the opponent's changes without letting him detect your moves.

Chapter 3

由著熟而漸悟懂勁，由懂勁而階及
神明，然非用力之久，不能豁然貫
通焉．

Translation:
To become proficient, regular practice will lead to a gradual understanding of the power of Chi. From understanding such power one will slowly advance to the point of excellence. If one does not practise long enough one cannot fully acquire this knowledge.

Explanation:
The Tai Chi Chuan form is the structure and push hands is the application. One needs to practise consistently with dedication to reach perfection. Even with such regular practice, only through time will one reach the level of perfection.

虛靈頂勁，氣沉丹田．

Translation:
Empty the mind and straighten the neck so as to enable the Chi to sink to the Dan Tian point.

Explanation:
When practising the form or push hands, the neck should always be straightened so as to enable the *Chi* to flow and sink to the *Dan Tian* point through *Yi* (the intention of the mind). If *Chi* does not sink to the *Dan Tian* point, this is usually the result of blockage at certain meridian points in the body.

不偏不倚，忽隱忽現。

Translation:
Not leaning or inclining. Conceal and reveal unexpectedly.

Explanation:
When practising and applying Tai Chi Chuan, the posture should be upright and neither leaning nor inclining, as this affects one's balance and centre. "To conceal and reveal" refers to the ability to shift between substantial and insubstantial without being detected. Hence, when in combat, one should not reveal one's movements to the opponent.

左重則左虛，右重則右杳。

Translation:
When the weight is on the left, the left becomes empty. When the weight is on the right, the right becomes undetectable.

Explanation:
Weight means the force or power of the opponent's attack. Empty means the intercepting power used is invisible and cannot be gauged. These two phrases explain the meaning of concealing and revealing. When adhering to the opponent, the point of contact on the left becomes insubstantial or empty, when the pressure of the force is felt at that point. The same applies to the right side. To be undetectable when adhering one must follow the opponent and neutralise the power without the slightest resistance, causing the opponent to fall into emptiness and be unable to do anything about it. When attacked, one should anticipate with emptiness so that one does not counter the opponent's force with force. This allows one to

stick to the opponent and neutralise his force. Not applying the concept of emptiness allows your opponent to sense the direction of your movements and your strength, thus giving him the advantage to counteract your move.

仰之則彌高，俯之則彌深，進之則愈長，退之則愈促。

Translation:
When pushed upwards, one extends further up. When pushed downwards, one plunges down. When advancing one increases the distance. When retreating one accelerates.

Explanation:
When the opponent attacks upwards, one should extend upwards to stop the opponent reaching. If the opponent pushes downward, one should sink further, giving the opponent a sensation of falling down a bottomless pit. When the opponent moves forward, one creates the sense of unreachable distance. When the opponent retreats, one pursues, thus not allowing him to escape. These all refer to the ability to adhere, follow and not lose contact, thus making the opponent unable to manifest his power.

一羽不能加，蠅蟲不能落，人不知我，我獨知人，英雄所向無敵，蓋由此而及也。

Translation:
Cannot add the weight of a feather. A fly not able to alight. Others do not know me but I alone know others. One becomes invincible when one masters all these principles.

Explanation:
The first two phrases mean the ability to detect even a very light sensation such as a feather or a fly. When one acquires such a level of skill, one has reached a high level of sensitivity and nimbleness and can feel the very slightest touch. At such a high level of skill, movement is agile and light, hence, naturally the opponent will not be able to "detect" you, while you are able to "read" him.

斯技旁門者多，雖勢有區別，概不外壯欺弱，慢讓快耳，有力打無力，手慢讓手快，是皆先天自然之能，非關學力而有為也。

Translation:
There are various other branches of Wu Shu (Martial Arts) with their own differences. However they all emphasise strong physical strength overcoming the weak. The slow are overcome by the fast. Those with strength will defeat those without. Those who are slow will lose to the one who is faster. But this is a natural process and has no relation to the ability and knowledge of the person or to effectiveness of the art.

Explanation:
Self-explanatory

察四兩撥千斤，顯非力勝。

Translation:
A thousand pounds can be moved by four ounces.

Explanation:
This statement demonstrates the effectiveness of the principles of Tai Chi Chuan, such as neutralising and diverting, which are often used in its applications.

觀耄耋能禦眾之形，快何能為。

Translation:
To see an old man defend and humiliate a number of people. This cannot be done by speed alone.

Explanation:
This demonstrates the principle of adhering, to render the opponent powerless no matter how strong or fast he is.

立如平準，活似車輪。

Translation:
To stand upright and balanced. Move like a wheel.

Explanation:
To stand upright and balanced means suspending the head and raising one's spirit. Move like a wheel means using the waist as the axle to turn the other parts of the body.

偏沉則隨、雙重則滯。

Translation:
One's ability to shift and sink will allow one to follow, whereas double weighting will lead to sluggishness.

Explanation:
In the application of this concept, when two people of equal strength resist each other physically with force, this results in double weighting and stalemate. However, if one relaxes one's force slightly and sinks further, the opponent will be unable to exert any physical force as his physical force is easily neutralised. In most physical confrontation, the stronger is normally the winner, but not so in this case, when the principles of Tai Chi Chuan are applied.

每見數年純功不能運化者，率為人所制，雙重之病未悟耳．

Translation:
Often we see people practising for years who are unable to apply these principles. This is because they lack the understanding of Bing (or illness) of double weighting.

Explanation:
Refer to explanation for previous translation i.e. *"One's ability to shift and sink will allow one to follow, whereas double weighting will lead to sluggishness "*.

若欲避此病，須知陰陽．

Translation:
To avoid such illness, one must appreciate the importance of Yin and Yang.

Explanation:
Illness means double weighting. *Yin* and *Yang* means insubstantial and substantial. At the slightest feeling of double weighting in oneself, one must sink and move quickly to correct the mistake by being more substantial or insubstantial, depending on the given circumstances.

黏即是走，走即是黏，陰不離陽，
陽不離陰，陰陽相濟，方為懂勁。

Translation:
To adhere is to "flee". To "flee" is to adhere. Yin cannot be separated from Yang. And Yang cannot be separated from Yin. Yin and Yang both complement each other. This is the understanding of Chi power.

Explanation:
With the separation of *Yin* and *Yang*, one should adhere and link without breaking off. To be able to adhere leads to the ability to "flee" i.e. neutralise. The interchanges between *Yin* and *Yang* cannot be defined but both complement each other and depend solely on the intention of the opponent. When one can deal with substantial and insubstantial without missing a small fraction, then one can be considered to have mastered the concept of *Dong Jin* (i.e. understanding the essence of the power).

懂勁後，愈練愈精，默識揣摩，漸
至從心所欲。

Translation:
When one understands the power of Jin, more practice leads to more refinement. To know the concept of Jin by heart enables one to continuously fathom out the true essence. Gradually, one will achieve what one desires.

Explanation:
Once *Jin* has been understood, one can be considered as having crossed the threshold. One must not break the continuity of daily

practice, and should reflect on every movement. Each finding should be borne in mind. The body follows the intention of the mind without hindrance. Through such process, one gradually refines and masters the skills over time.

本是捨己隨人、多誤舍近求遠。

Translation:
Basically, the idea is to abandon oneself and follow the opponent. Many have mistakenly abandoned the near to seek the far.

Explanation:
In general, the concept of Tai Chi Chuan is that of following the opponent rather than taking the initiative. For every movement there is a direction. It is this direction that you seek, try to adhere to, and follow without resistance. This results in the opponent missing the target without realising that he is overstretched or using excessive force. If one sticks regularly to a sequence of hand techniques instead of applying the concept of adhering and following, this means abandoning the near and seeking the far.

斯謂差之毫釐，謬之千里，學者不可不詳辨焉。

Translation:
There is a saying that "missing by an inch leads to missing the target by a thousand miles". Practitioners must try to understand this concept exactly.

Explanation:
When adhering to and linking with the opponent, one must deal

with him at the point of contact. This is referred to as "not missing by an inch". Any parting from the point of contact becomes a lost opportunity and hence missing the target by "a thousand miles".

此論句句切要，並無一字敷衍陪襯，非有夙慧，不能悟也，先師不肯妄傳，非獨擇人，亦恐枉費功夫矣．

Translation :
Every sentence in this Old Manual is important. There is not a single word of "flowery talk". Without natural ability one will have great difficulty in understanding. The teacher is reluctant to pass on his knowledge except to the chosen ones, in order not to waste his time and effort.

Explanation:
The intricacies of Tai Chi Chuan are all within this old manual. Those without a natural ability will not be able to understand. One can thus see that this art cannot be viewed as an acrobatic form.

Chapter 4

陳微明
太極拳論

Chen Wei Ming's
Tai Chi Quan Lun

The idea of practising martial arts is to strengthen the body (i.e. muscle and bones), to balance the *Chi* and blood circulation, to harmonise the body, mind and spirit and to prevent ill health and acquire longevity. It is an ancient system used to cultivate good health.

Tai Chi Chuan is based on principles of movement and stillness and changes occurring from substantial to insubstantial, with an emphasis on upright and relaxed postures. The movements are agile, light and circular in motion. Hence, when one part of the body moves every part moves, or when one part is still, every part is still. This is similar to Taoist meditation in principle.

From the martial point of view, Tai Chi Chuan is regarded as an internal style because it comes from the same principle of Taoism. People of all ages and either gender can practise it. It is a very natural and painless form of exercise that has no adverse effects on health.

If one practises regularly with commitment, over time one can reap the benefits of health to the body, mind and spirit.

Chapter 5

打手歌

Da Shou Ge

The Song of Push Hands

Da Shou Ge
(Song One)

掤握擠按須認真
上下相隨人難進
任他巨力來打我
牽動四兩撥千斤
引進滿空合即出
粘連綿隨不丟頂

Translation:

One needs to be clear and precise when executing the postures of Peng, Lu, Ji and An, through co-ordination of the upper and lower body movements. The opponent will encounter difficulty in finding the weakness and breaking through one's defence. Whatever the strength or force used by the opponent, one needs only four ounces to shift a thousand pounds. Entice the opponent into emptiness and immediately close the structure to repel him. Continually stick lightly and follow without losing contact or resisting the opponent.

Explanation:

掤擺擠按須認真

One needs to be clear and precise when executing the postures of Peng, Lu, Ji and An

Clear and precise means one should follow the teacher's instructions and the principles regarding the usage of the basic four postures.

上下相隨人難進
任他巨力來打我
牽動四兩撥千斤

Through co-ordination of the upper and lower movements, the opponent will encounter difficulty in finding the weakness and breaking through one's defence. Whatever the strength or force used by the opponent, one needs only four ounces to shift a thousand pounds.

Daily practice of push hands incorporating the right principles and concepts will help you develop the co-ordination of upper and lower body movements naturally.

When attacked, any small movements are detected through *Ting Jin* (or listening energy). As soon as the opponent makes a move, whatever strength or power is used can be neutralised or deflected by using a very small force.

引進滿空合即出

Entice the opponent to enter into emptiness and close the structure to repel him instantly.

If the opponent attacks with a powerful force, it is usually straight and extended from a distance. Whilst in motion, he cannot change the direction of attack. One can then lead the direction of attack, to entice him into emptiness. The concept of enticing into emptiness means to steer the flow of attack away from the body without the opponent knowing or sensing the change in direction. In the opponent's mind, he is still thinking that he is on target.

粘連綿隨不丟頂

Continually stick lightly and follow without losing contact or resisting the opponent.

In order to achieve this, one must develop the skill and ability to adhere and follow the opponent's movements without losing contact, and not try to resist the force applied by the opponent, such as by counteracting force with force.

Chapter 5

Da Shou Ge
(Song Two)

彼不動，己不動
彼微動，己先動
似鬆非鬆，將展未展
勁斷意不斷

Translation:
*One does not move if the opponent does not move.
Any small movement initiated by the opponent,
one would have already made a move.
One's movement might appear to look
loose but in fact it is not.
One is preparing to expand but is not yet expanding.
Even with a break in Jin,
the Yi still persists.*

Explanation:

彼不動，己不動
彼微動，己先動

One does not move if the opponent does not move.
Any small movement initiated by the opponent, one would have already made a move.

In *Tui Shou* (or push hands), when the opponent does not move, one remains still and anticipates any advancement from him. Any movements made are directional. However, one's intention will always be ahead of the opponent's action and will move in advance in response to the direction accordingly. As soon as the opponent moves, he will be immobilised and thrown.

似鬆非鬆，將展未展
勁斷意不斷

One's movement might appear to look loose but in fact it is not.
One is preparing to expand but is not yet expanding.
Even with a break in Jin, the Yi (intention of the mind) still persists.

All this action involves the use of *Ting Jin* (or Listening Energy). One is always in readiness to seek the opportunity. As soon as it arises, the energy is applied through the continuation of *Yi*, even though the movement may have ended.

Chapter 6

楊澄甫
太極拳十要

Yang Cheng Fu's Ten Principles of Tai Chi Chuan

Yang Cheng Fu's Ten Principles of Tai Chi Chuan

一　虛靈頂勁
二　含胸拔背
三　鬆腰
四　分虛實
五　沉肩墜肘
六　用意不用力
七　上下相隨
八　內外相合
九　相連不斷
十　動中求靜

虛靈頂勁
(Xu Ling Ding Jin)

Translation:
Emptying the thoughts and raising the head as if the crown of the head is pressed up against the heaven.

The neck must be straightened to allow the head to be raised and vertical. This allows the spirit and *Chi* to arrive at the crown of the head. No physical strength should be used, as physical force will cause stiffness and also hinder the blood and *Chi* circulation. One must have natural intention of emptiness in the mind.

含胸拔背
(Han Xiong Ba Bei)

Translation:
Hollowing the chest to raise the back.

Hollowing the chest will help to sink the *Chi* down to the *Dan Tian* point. It is imperative not to expand the chest as this will raise the *Chi* to the chest, causing top heaviness and the heels to lift. To raise the back is to allow the *Chi* to adhere to the back. If one hollows the chest the back will rise naturally. With the back raised, one can project the *Chi* from the spine.

鬆腰
(Song Yao)

Translation:
Loosening up the waist.

The waist is the commander of the body. When one is able to loosen up the waist, this will increase *Chi* energy in both legs and thus provide a stable base for firm rooting. Changes from substantial to insubstantial or vice-versa are derived from the movement of the waist. There is a saying that the source of *Chi* energy is from the waist, therefore if one lacks strength, one should pay more attention to the waist and the lower limbs.

分虛實
(Fen Xu Shi)

Translation:
Distinguishing between substantial and insubstantial.

When one's weight is on the right, the right leg becomes substantial and the left leg insubstantial, or vice versa. When one is able to distinguish the difference, one will be able to turn and move with lightness and effortlessness. If not, any steps will be sluggish and unstable and can easily be unbalanced by others.

沉肩墜肘
(Chen Lian Zhu Zhou)

Translation:
Sinking the shoulder and weighting down the elbow.

Sinking the shoulder is to let the shoulder loosen up and drop downwards. If not, both shoulders will rise causing *Chi* to rise with them. No strength can be exerted from the body if this happens. Weighting down the elbow is to let the elbow drop and hang loose. If the elbow is raised, the shoulders will have great difficulty in sinking, thus affecting the strength of your internal power, and you will not be able to throw the opponent away. This is similar to what is known as "stifling the power" in external martial arts.

用意不用
(Yong Yi Bu Yong Li)

Translation:
Using Yi or intention and not physical strength.

For practitioners of Tai Chi Chuan, the whole body must be relaxed so that no physical strength remains within the sinews and bones to restrict one's power. Only then will one be light and flexible, and move accordingly. One might doubt how one could develop such power without using physical strength. It is because the human body contains meridians, which enable the flow of *Chi*. When physical strength is used, this will cause the blockage of *Chi* in these meridians and result in sluggish movements. Any movement in a small part of the body will affect the whole body. Using the mind or *Yi*, *Chi* will flow to where it is directed. It also helps the flow of both blood and *Chi* circulation and strengthens the body.

上下相隨
(Shang Xia Xiang Sui)

Translation:
Co-ordination of both the upper and lower body.

In accordance to Tai Chi Chuan theory, rooting is from the legs, the command from the waist and expression through the hands. From legs to waist, there needs to be unison of movement. The movements of hands, waist and legs will also be followed by the intention in the eyes. This is regarded as the complete co-ordination of above and below. If one of these is missing, the move becomes fragmented.

內外相合
(Nei Wai Xiang Ge)

Translation:
Internal and external in togetherness.

The training of Tai Chi Chuan is in the spirit, hence spirit is the commander-in-chief and the body will move as directed. When the spirit is raised and movements become light, the form consists of open and close - open means not only opening the hands and legs but also includes the mind within it. When closing, it should be the same. Therefore, there is no gap between the external and internal and they should be in unison.

相連不斷
(Xiang Lian Bu Duan)

Translation:
Continuity without breakage.

In external martial arts, the power used is only physical strength and therefore there is a start and finish to it. In between is the break where the strength from the previous move is finished and before new force is issued, which is the weakest point and can be easily exploited by the opponent. Tai Chi Chuan uses *Yi* and not physical strength, hence the move becomes continuous without ending, like a roaring river without ceasing. When in circulation, the *Chi* is described as like drawing silk from a cocoon, to signify the continuous flow of movement.

動中求靜
(Dong Zhong Qiu Jing)

Translation:
Seeking stillness within movement.

In external martial arts, the power is generated by jumping, punching and kicking as hard as possible. Hence after prolonged practice, one is panting for breath and at times the blood vessels are enlarged. By contrast, Tai Chi Chuan emphasises stillness over movement. Even though in motion, the form appears to be tranquil. Therefore when practising, the slower the better, with long deep breathing, to allow the *Chi* to sink to the *Dan Tian* point and thus prevent one from over-exerting oneself physically.

Right:
Sword application as demonstrated by Grandmaster Ip and Great Grandmaster Yang. Picture taken in 1965

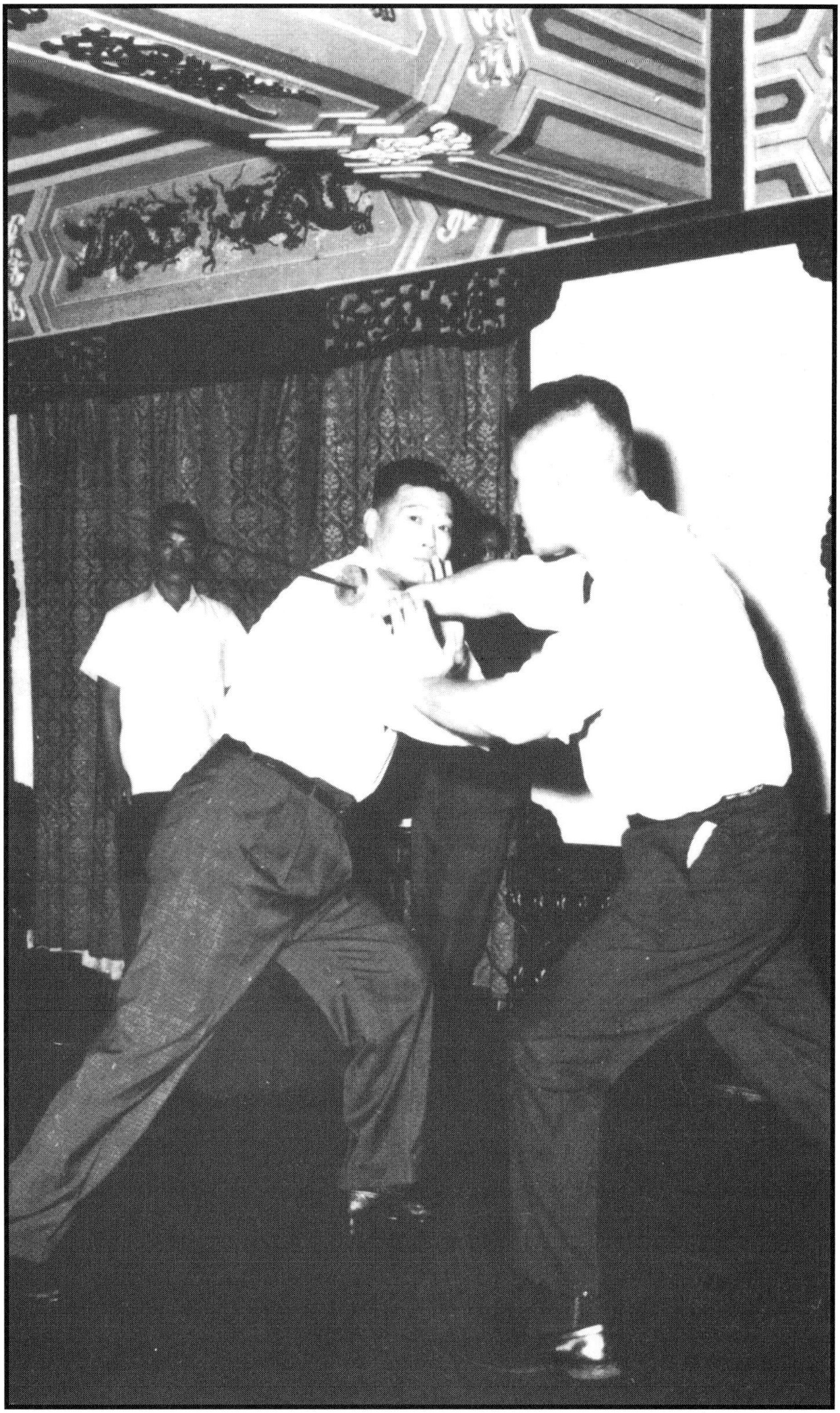

Chapter 7

五行要義詳解

Explanation of the Essence of the Five Elements

In Chinese, the Five Elements refer to:

金　**Jin** *(metal)*

木　**Mu** *(wood)*

水　**Shui** *(water)*

火　**Huo** *(fire)* and

土　**Tu** *(earth)*

The Chi powers related to the five elements are:

粘　**Nian** *(touching)*

連　**Lian** *(linking or joining)*

黏　**Nian** *(adhering)*

隨　**Sui** *(following)* and

不丟頂　**Bu Diu Ding** *(not confronting or disengaging)*

1. Nian *(Touching)*　粘

When one person lifts the other through contact of touching, this is referred to as a form of *Jin* in Tai Chi Chuan terms. This *Jin* does not stick to or lift the person directly but is induced indirectly through *Yi*. In push hands or in combat, when the opponent is strong both physically and internally with firm rooting, it is difficult to lift or shift his centre. If one uses *Nian*, one can make the opponent lose his balance and with the addition of intention, one can draw the opponent's attention and energy to the upper part of his body resulting in automatically severing his rooting. This is caused by the opponent's reaction to the application of *Nian*. At this instance, one can let go and entice the opponent into emptiness. This is referred to as *Nian* or touching.

Another example is that of basketball. One can see a professional basketball player able to hold and manipulate the ball with the fingers easily by just gently touching and pressing slightly downwards on the surface of the ball. This is the result of the rebound force of the ball from the floor. *Nian* (or touching) can thus also be used to initiate a move.

Use the principle of intention (as mentioned above) or envisaging to attack the opponent where he is most unsuspecting and unprepared. Even though the opponent is strong and well defended and not afraid of being attacked with any intensity of physical force, he is vulnerable to deception. If one can entice the opponent to relinquish defence and focus on attack, this will cause the forces to split up thus diminishing the consolidated forces of the opponent. One can then attack the diminishing forces one at a time. This is to entice the opponent to initiate the move and then destroy him through his error. It is said that one should attack when the opponent is not defending, and not initiate an attack when he is defending. In time, practitioners will gain better insight into the use of *Nian* or intention.

2. Lian *(Linking)* 連

The move should be projected through without breaking or becoming disjointed. All the joints should be linked together without breakage or ending. No pausing or intermission, like stringing the nine crocked pearls. This allows the circulation of *Chi* throughout the body.

3. Nian (*Adhering*) 黏

The process of adhering is always in response to the direction of the opponent's force. For example, when the force is coming forward, you move back without losing the contact of adhering, or when the opponent retreats, you keep the contact by advancing forward. When applying the principle of adhering, you should always move with the flow without letting the opponent break loose, and not resist the opponent's direction of force.

4. Sui *(Following)* 隨

Sui means not to take the initiative but just to follow the opponent's movement. In any situation, you should always keep pace with the opponent in terms of speed, advancement or retreat. Only then will you be able to keep the opponent under control, as you are able to anticipate his every move.

5. Bu Diu Ding 不丟頂
(Neither confronting nor disengaging)

To confront is to resist. To disengage is to lose contact or separate. Do not break contact, confront, rush your response and/or lag behind.

This is the source of the five elements and the basis of agility.

太極拳十三勢大義

The Meaning of the Thirteen Tai Chi Chuan Postures

The thirteen Tai Chi Chuan postures are based on the principle of the five elements and the eight trigrams. In push hands practice, there are therefore thirteen ways of *Jin* (or issuing power).

五行 **Wu Hang** (Five Elements) comprise:

進 **Jin** *(Advancing)*

退 **Tui** *(Stepping back)*

顧 **Gu** *(Being attentive)*

盼 **Pan** *(Gazing)*

定 **Ding** *(Being still)*

This can be further subdivided into an internal and an external aspect:

External Aspect:
Jin is advancing
Tui is retreating
Gu is being attentive on your left
Pan is keeping an eye to the right
Ding is being rooted and stable.

Internal Aspect:
Jin is touching and entering
Tui is linking

Gu is adhering
Pan is *Sui* (i.e. following and yielding)
Ding is not resisting or losing contact.

八卦 Ba Gua
(Eight Trigrams)

This can be explained by both external and internal concepts.

External:

四正四偶
Si Zheng Si Ou
(The four directions and four corners).

These are regarded as the positions.

Internal:

| 掤 Peng | 擄 Lu | 擠 Ji | 按 An |
| 採 Cai | 裂 Lie | 肘 Zhou | 靠 Kao |

These are regarded as *Jin* power.

All practitioners use the form for practising and push hands for application. The classics state that the power is rooted at the feet, derived from the legs, controlled from the waist and expressed through the fingers. All practitioners must be fully aware of this. This is the essence of Tai Chi Chuan.

Chapter 8

太極拳慢與
不用力之解釋

Explanation of the Slow Movement Without Physical Strength in Tai Chi Chuan Practice

Chinese proverb:

慢工出細貨

(Man Gong Chu Xi Huo)

Translation:

Slow work produces detail and quality goods.

Many doubt the usefulness and power of Tai Chi Chuan because of its slow movement and because it does not rely on the use of physical strength. However, Tai Chi Chuan can in fact be extremely effective - but only if one first studies the principles. Only when one understands these principles can one then learn the method. When one becomes proficient with the method, one can then apply it. If one is unable to apply Tai Chi Chuan, this is only because one has not practised the art to a sufficient standard. For example the process of making steel first starts with pig iron, which then becomes wrought iron before being turned into steel. This takes a long process of treatment before it reaches the required stage. When practising Tai Chi Chuan, one has to be relaxed and natural. The emphasis is on intention rather than using physical strength or holding the breath. Such actions will cause one to be sluggish and cumbersome. Hence, it is important to sink the *Chi* to the *Dan Tian* and keep the body relaxed.

以靜制動
(Yi Jing Zhi Dong)

Translation :

Tai Chi Chuan uses calmness to subdue agitation.

以柔制剛
(Yi Rou Zhi Gang)

Translation:

Tai Chi Chuan uses softness to overcome rigidity.

From nothingness, something emerges. To have is not to have. Substantial as if insubstantial. Accepting what comes your way, without losing contact or resistance. These are all interchanges derived from the concept of substantial and insubstantial in Tai Chi Chuan. Slowness means taking time and allowing oneself to calm down, thus enabling oneself to defend. To defend is to settle down, which involves sinking and settling the *Chi*. To settle down leads to calmness, thus enabling one to relax. When the spirit is relaxed, one can sink the *Chi* and thus feel refreshed and energised, with a focused mind. Slowness is due to observance. With the observing mind, there is clarity within the spirit and hence any sluggishness in the *Chi* is eliminated. Speed is due to oversight resulting from impatience. Impatience causes the *Chi* to rise. With the *Chi* floating high, impatience leads to unsettledness. There is no focusing and this brings about weakness, as a result of dispersed *Chi*. There is no agility. To be calm and to use softness, to overcome agitation and rigidity are all from sensing. Hence the Tai Chi Chuan form is to train the body and mind, while push hands is to work on the applications.

The initial stage of practising push hands is to train the sensitivity of the mind through the body to allow the sensing of every little movement, so that one can anticipate the changes of the opponent's intention. This can only be experienced within the mind and cannot be described in words. Any changes taking place are derived from the quickness of one's sensation and therefore derive from an understanding of the concept of substantial and insubstantial. This is what is meant by slow movement without any physical strength.

Chapter 9

太極拳
十三要點

Thirteen Essential Points of Tai Chi Chuan

13 Essential Points of Tai Chi Chuan.

1. 氣沉丹田

   Sinking the *Chi* to the *Dan Tian* point

2. 涵胸拔背

   Hollowing the chest to raise the back

3. 虛靈頂勁

   Emptying the thoughts and raising the head as if the crown of the head is pressed up against the heaven

4. 沉肩垂肘

   Sinking the shoulder and weighting down the elbow

5. 分虛實

   Distinguishing between substantial and insubstantial

6. 鬆腰胯

   Loosening up the waist

7. 用意不用力

   Using *Yi* (or intention) and not physical strength

8. 上下相隨

   The co-ordination of both the upper and lower body

9. 意氣相連

   Chi and *Yi* linked together

10. 內外相合

    Internal and external in togetherness

11. 動中求靜

    Seeking stillness within movement

12. 動靜合一

    Combining movement and stillness as one

13. 式式均勻

    Seeking evenness in every movement

Right:
Grandmaster Ip uses "Hua Jin" to neutralise the opponent's force (picture taken in the late sixties)

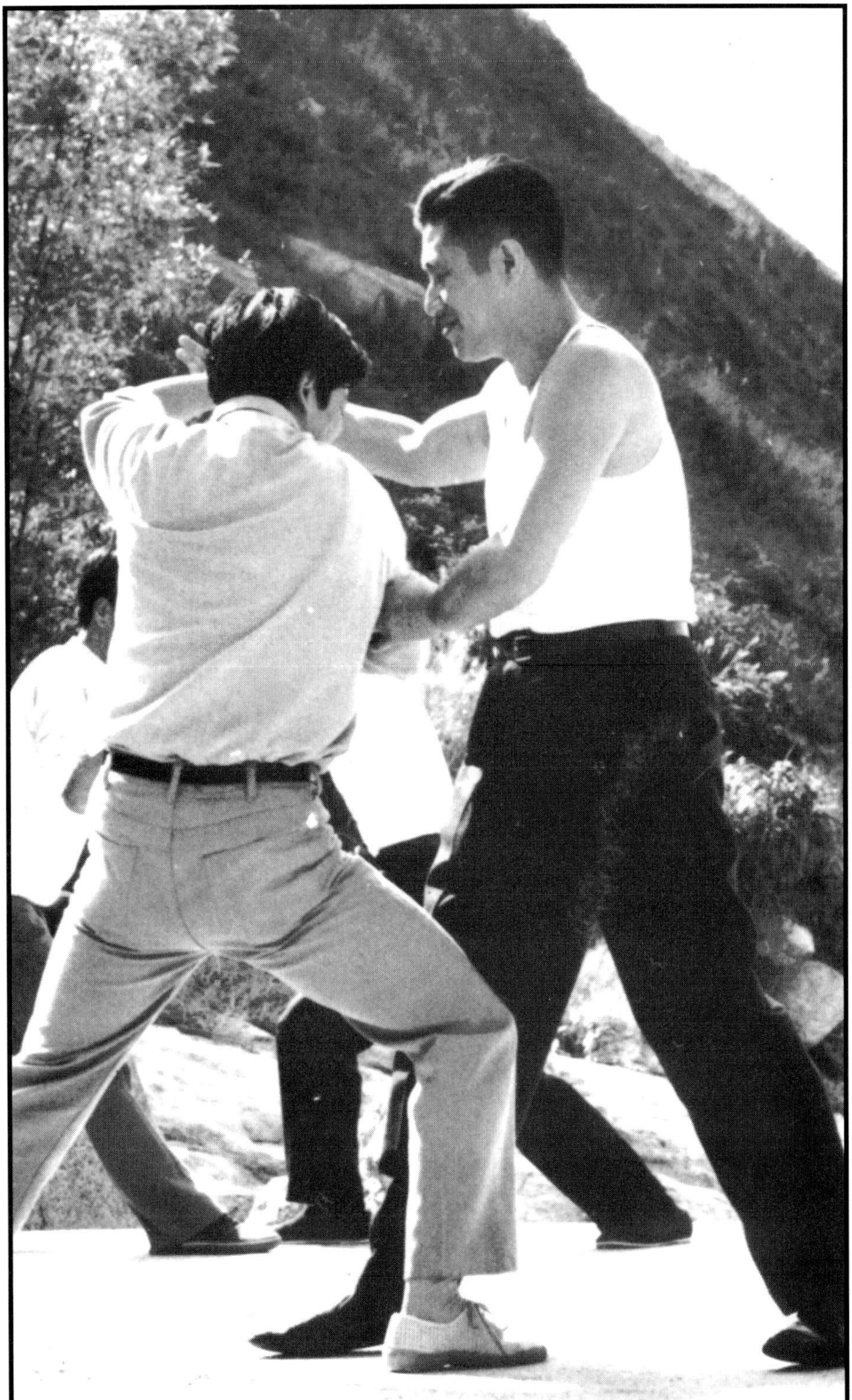

Chapter 10

太極拳十二病

Twelve Illnesses in Tai Chi Chuan

Also known as
Twelve Common Mistakes
made when practising
Tai Chi Chuan

Twelve Weaknesses in Tai Chi Chuan

1. 俯 頭
   Dropping the head

2. 曲 項
   Bending the neck

3. 露 肩
   Lifting or tensing the shoulders

4. 揚 肘
   Protruding the elbows

5. 駝 背
   Hunching the back

6. 凹 胸
   Crouching

7. 鼓 腰
   Forced extension of the stomach

8. 撅 臀
   Lifting the buttocks

9. 指 胯
   Not tucking the hips at the joints

10. 憋柱
    Tightening the coccyx

11. 直膝
    Locking up the knees

12. 歪腳
    Incorrect foot positioning

Apart from all these above, there are also:

♦ too much straightness or stiffness of the waist

♦ closing the space at the armpit

♦ use of physical strength

♦ use of physical force when breathing

♦ holding the breath at the chest

All these severe faults are detrimental to your Tai Chi Chuan development.

Right:
Tai Chi Chuan Self-defence
by Grandmaster Ip (taken in the 70's)

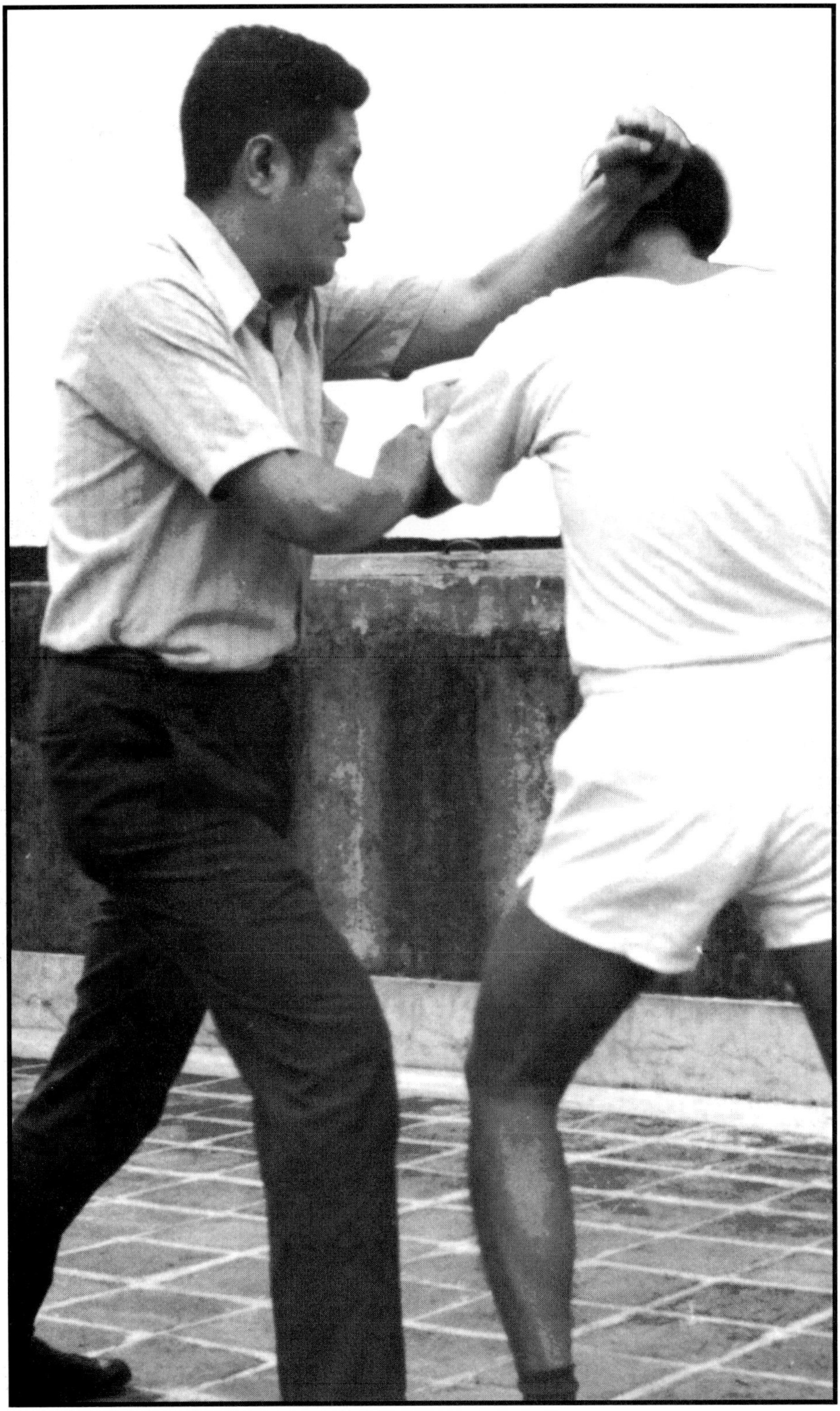

Chapter 11

太極拳

十二正

Twelve Essential Elements of Tai Chi Chuan

These twelve essential elements are structured on three areas of the body, namely the shoulders, chest and legs:

1. **Shoulders**

    - both shoulders should be balanced and in alignment

    i) Body should be squared

    ii) Shoulders sunk and relaxed

    iii) Elbows weighted down

    iv) Wrists smooth and straight

2. **Chest**

    - hollowing the chest

    i) Head is suspended from above

    ii) Back is raised

    iii) Waist is relaxed and loose

    iv) Abdomen is without tension

3. **Legs**

    - both legs must be co-ordinated

    i) Crotch (i.e. inner legs region) must be opened and rounded

    ii) Knees must be bent

    iii) Footwork must be soft and agile

    iv) Differentiate between substantial and insubstantial

Apart from the above, the following points should also be observed:
1. The *Kua* (hip joints) should be flexible
2. The knees should be rotated outwardly

3. The knees should be pointing downwards
4. Sink the *Chi* to the *Dan Tian* point
5. There should be a folding line at the navel around the waist
6. The vertebrae two inches above the coccyx should be flexible and move with every movement
7. The area around the shoulder blades should be rounded and extended.
8. All movements should be directed by the waist

The sinking of *Chi* to the *Dan Tian* point is extremely important. If this is not achieved, the basis of Tai Chi Chuan will not be realised. From the sinking of *Chi* to the *Dan Tian* point, one can square the body, loosen the waist and increase the flexibility of the *Kua*. This will enable one to move or turn easily with rooting. In addition, it also allows

i) the feet to be more relaxed, balanced, centred and rooted

ii) the body to be more relaxed with a better flow of *Chi* energy to allow one to draw the energy without any breakage in flow, as if drawing silk from a cocoon.

iii) to be able to assess and capitalise on an opportunity i.e. to deal with both strengths and weaknesses of the opponent.

The concept of sinking the *Chi* at the *Dan Tian* must not be overlooked. This is a very important aspect of Tai Chi Chuan.

Right:
Grandmaster Ip and Master Ding demonstrating push hands technique (taken in 1999)

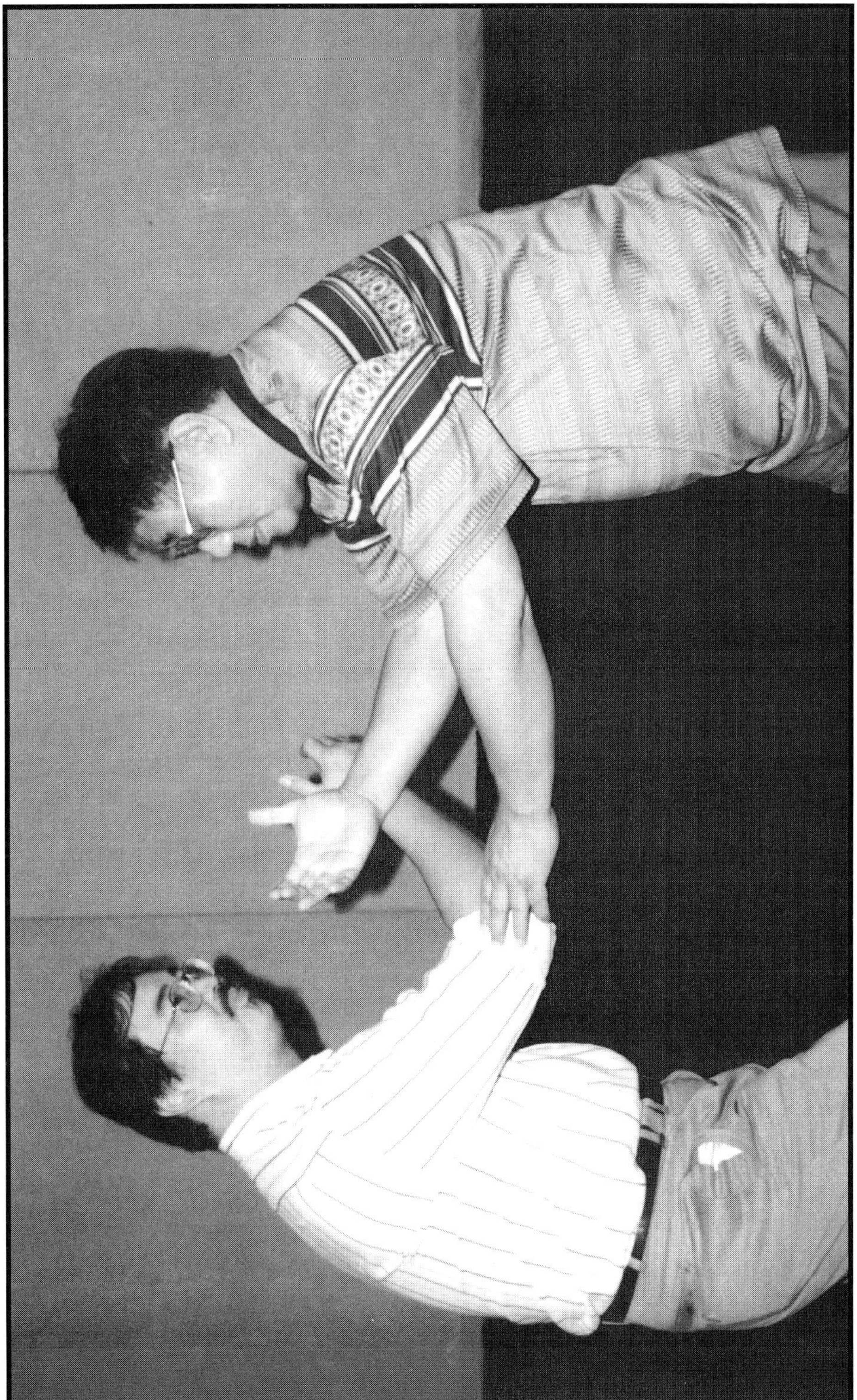

Chapter 12

武當拳節錄

Extract from Wudang Gong Fu Series

Extract from Wudang Gong Fu Series

何謂太極？
What is Tai Chi Chuan?

The principles developed from Tai Chi Chuan are based on Taoist philosophy and use a natural way of overpowering physical strength, enabling one to use minimal force to overcome strength, and slowness to overcome speed. This can be explained through a scientific approach.

無力打有力
Use of minimal force to overcome strong physical strength.

According to the principles of mechanics, any force will have a spiral motion incorporated with pivoting action to allow pulling and dragging. For example when a train derails, in order to restore the train back on to the track, a jacking device is used to lift the train. The device can be operated by simply using a spiral turning motion, which requires minimal force. This clearly demonstrates the concept of applying minimal force to move heavier weights. The theory in Tai Chi Chuan classics describes this concept as drawing silk from a cocoon through a continuous spiral motion, following a state of flux. This then allows the principles of both pulling and dragging to be applied with ease. This is the same as the concept of:

以曲取直
"Yi Qu Qiu Zhi"
i.e. the use of a spiralling motion to overcome linear force and

以柔克剛
"Yi Rou Ke Gang"
i.e. the use of softness to overpower hardness.

手慢打手快
The slow overcoming the fast.

According to the principles of mechanics, centrifugal force is most effective because it comes from the centre. If we consider a wheel of a three feet radius with a foot radius shaft in the centre, when the wheel shaft turns 45 degrees, the inside wheel only turns through a circular distance of less than 4 inches. The external wheel will travel through a circular distance of more than a foot. Therefore, there is a ratio of 1:3. For three turns at the centre, the outside wheel turns one revolution. Hence using the waist as the centre, applying the same principle using "time dimension", the distance travelled in a second at the centre will cause the circumference to travel a greater distance. In the above example, it would be three times the distance. The Tai Chi Chuan classics emphasise using the waist like the shaft of a turning wheel, which follows the principle of the slow overcoming the fast. This can be further expanded in the following usage of Tai Chi Chuan postures:

1. Lu Jin *(or Roll Back Energy)* 履 勁

Using the concept of the motion of the wheel in order to spin the opponent round effectively, the presence of contact friction is also required. This is the principle of *Lu Jin*.

Extract from Wudang Gong Fu Series

2. Peng Jin *(or Ward Off Energy)* 掤勁

If the opponent puts on pressure, there is a danger of the spiral force being compressed and distorted, hence making it difficult to turn. To resist such pressure or to avoid the force being distorted, sometimes hard physical resistance is used so that the spiralling turn is inhibited. In order to avoid this, one must utilise the principle of "hardness within softness". Hence when two forces meet, the softness outside will provide a spring cushion to allow spiralling to take place. This is the characteristic of *Peng Jin* or Ward Off power.

3. Ji Jin *(or Press Energy)* 擠勁

If one comes in contact with a strong physical resistance, one needs to increase the amount of ward off power in order to be able to spiral through. To increase the amount of ward off power is to use both hands, warding off in different directions but meeting at the centre of the opponent's force. This is the *Ji Jin*.

4. An Jin *(or Push Energy)* 按勁

Because the root is at the feet, in order to turn or move the root or to spiral in and turn the opponent's body, the effective way is to spiral downwards at an angle. This will impose a lifting motion within a focused area to get a reaction without the opponent breaking free (i.e. the concept of sticking is applied). This is *An Jin*.

5. Cai Jin *(or Pull Energy)* 採勁

Sometimes one cannot make out the opponent's direction of force. In this situation, one has to apply *Cai Jin* to bring out the opponent's force. *Cai Jin* comprises two separating forces in opposing directions and is the reverse of *Ji Jin*. *Cai Jin* can be applied for different purposes such as grabbing or breaking depending on the position. Once the opponent's force is drawn out, you can then either *Nian* (touch) or *Nian* (adhere) and when the opponent moves, then you should *Lian* (link) and *Sui* (follow), to follow every reaction of your opponent. To be able to execute *Nian, Lian, Nian and Sui*, one must understand the concept of substantial and insubstantial to allow changes to occur in response to any body movements and to seize any opportunities (For further explanation of Nian, Lian, Nian and Sui, refer to Chapter 14).

There are four ways to supplement *Nian, Lian, Nian* and *Sui*, namely:

1. **Kong** (or to discharge)   空

2. **Jie** (or to complement another person's force)   結

3. **Cuo** (or to dampen or foil)   挫

4. **Rou** (or to knead)   揉

All these four principles are concealed within the coiling and uncoiling action. Coiling is to transform a big circle to a small circle and uncoiling is vice versa. Both these actions will cause a responsive reaction from the opponent through one's application of sinking and diverting. When the coiling and uncoiling reaches its ultimate stage, this final point is referred to as "storing *Chi* for releasing" i.e. a state of readiness for the power to be released. Because of the different directions of such applications, different names are given such as "roll" and "shift". Similarly this coiling / uncoiling can also be applied to the process of releasing power, with names such as "split", "elbow" and "shoulders". The action of storing the essence of power is initiated from the waist, back and knees. The use of centrifugal force helps to increase the potency of the springiness. Similarly, power is released by using the waist, back and the movement of the *Kua*, which are all directed to the opponent's centre, as in releasing an arrow from a bow. When carrying out these movements, the body must be upright and centred. This will enable one to weigh and assess the opponent's strength and direction. This storing action is usually referred to as *Dong Jin* or understanding of the essence of power.

To analyse Tai Chi Chuan from a scientific point of view, there are six approaches :

1. Centrifugal force plays the main role in the movements of Tai Chi Chuan.

2. Rifling motion (i.e. the spinning motion of a bullet shot from a rifled barrel) is the line of movement in Tai Chi Chuan.

3. Abrasion and springiness is the strength of attack and defence in Tai Chi Chuan.

4. Shifting the centre is the power generation process in Tai Chi Chuan.

5. Coiling to store and uncoiling to release is the strategy and weapon in Tai Chi Chuan.

6. Force towards the centre is the direction of attack in Tai Chi Chuan

There are in existence numerous different styles of Tai Chi Chuan. It is often difficult for beginners to find a good teacher for instruction. Fortunately, Tai Chi Chuan was practised by

Extract from Wudang Gong Fu Series

intellectuals in the old days who wrote numerous texts which have been passed down and can be used as a guide. Reading such texts will provide one with a better insight and understanding of the principles and concepts of Tai Chi Chuan. Practising Tai Chi Chuan with reference to these texts will always keep one's training on the correct path in order to continue to improve one's level.

People often ask,
"How does one know what real Tai Chi Chuan is?"
This can simply be answered from the Tai Chi Chuan classics, which state:

*" If one practises according to the
principles and concepts of Tai Chi Chuan
and is able to reap the benefits,
then it is true Tai Chi Chuan.
Such benefits may vary at
different levels - basic to advanced ".*

Right:
Grandmaster Ip demonstrating the application of the Tai Chi Chuan posture, " Chin Pu Tsai Chui"

125

Chapter 13

太極拳
三步審查法

**Tai Chi Chuan
Posture Checking**

Three-Step Method of Posture Examination

The Tai Chi Chuan Classics embody hidden meanings within the script and are often easily misinterpreted and misunderstood. This causes confusion for practitioners when they refer to the scripts for their training. To assist practitioners in the interpretation of the Tai Chi Chuan Classics, the essence of various scripts has been condensed and put into simple layman terms and a three-step method of examining the postures is used.

1. Shen *(Body)* 身

The body must be upright, relaxed and able to hold against pressure from all directions. The coccyx is straight and the spirit rises to the top through suspending the head. Any distortion in the body alignment will result in weakness. With correct body alignment, the effect is like a cartwheel, which can rotate in any direction. This is the posture of Tai Chi Chuan. With an upright body, there will be no stiffness in the waist and hence one will be relaxed and flexible. Such a posture will enable one to have the *Peng Jin* (ward off) power to hold against any incoming force from all directions.

There are various criteria for a correct posture, for example:

    a. **Lou Hsih Au Pu** 摟膝拗步
       (Brush Knee and Push)
       - check that the body is not leaning forward

    b. **Yue Fung Shih Pi** 如封似閉
       (Apparent Close Up and Push)
       - ensure that the body is not leaning backwards

    c. **Yeh Ma Fun Tsung** 野馬分鬃
       (Parting the Horse's Mane)
       - the body must not lean sideways

Chapter 13

   d. **Tan Pein Hsia Shih** 單鞭下勢
   (Snake Creeps Down)
   - when crouching, the body should not be leaning

If one makes any of the errors above, one has not attained the correct postures of Tai Chi Chuan.

2. Xing *(Expression)* 形

In Tai Chi Chuan classics, it is mentioned that the expression of Tai Chi Chuan movements is like an eagle catching its prey, and the spirit is like a cat about to pounce on a mouse. To raise the spirit, one should ensure that the mind and breath are activated without incurring any weakness in one's structure. All these are expressed from within.

In practising Tai Chi Chuan, the spirit must always be focused and alive. If this spirit is missing, the concentration is dispersed and the eyes are without focus or expression. The movements are without definition. If the face and eyes are obstructed by the hand movements or the hands lead the movement of the eyes, one cannot see beyond the hands. Therefore, there is no expression of the spirit in the movement. Without the spirit, the mind and breathing cannot be aroused and there is no generation and exchange of power. Hence, when practising Tai Chi Chuan, one must always ask the following questions:

A. Has the spirit been raised?

B. Is the spirit alive as if a cat is about to pounce on a mouse?

When one fulfils the above criteria, one is said to have acquired the concept of *Xing*.

3. Yao *(Waist)* 腰

Tai Chi classics refer to the *Yao* (waist) as the wheel shaft or as the banner. They also mention raising the spirit to the head, generating the power around the waist and making the root at the feet. In addition, one should pay attention to the waist to enable the abdomen to be relaxed, to generate *Chi* energy. All this emphasises the importance of the *yao* as it is the prime mover in advancing, stepping back, and moving left or right, which is also the principle of the slow overcoming the fast. When practising, always check whether the movement is initiated from the waist and also whether the region between the waist and coccyx is upright and straight.

For example:

a. **Pao Hu Kwei Shan** 抱虎歸山
   (Embrace the tiger and return to the mountain)
   - ensure that the power derives from the turn of the waist

b. **Pe Shen Chui** 撇身捶
   (Punch and parry)
   - ensure that the sinking power is derived from the turning of the waist

c. **Yu Nu Chuen Shu** 玉女穿梭
   (Fair lady throws shuttle)
   - ensure the relaxed power is derived from the waist

d. **Chuan Shen Pai Lien** 轉身擺蓮
   (Turn body to sweep lotus)
   - ensure the power of the legs comes from the waist

All the above are to do with movements initiated from the waist. When practising Tai Chi Chuan, the power is generated from turning the waist and not from any other part of the body. To achieve this, the waist must be relaxed without forcing any physical strength around it.

NOTE:

Any movements must first come from the waist followed by the hands and legs. The power used in the opening or closing postures must be hidden at the Kua region. When opening, the power is transferred from the Kua to the back and issued out. When closing, the power is stored at the Kua. These are the important criteria for generating power.

Right:
Great Grandmaster Yang and Grandmaster Ip demonstrating Tai Chi Chuan self-defence application

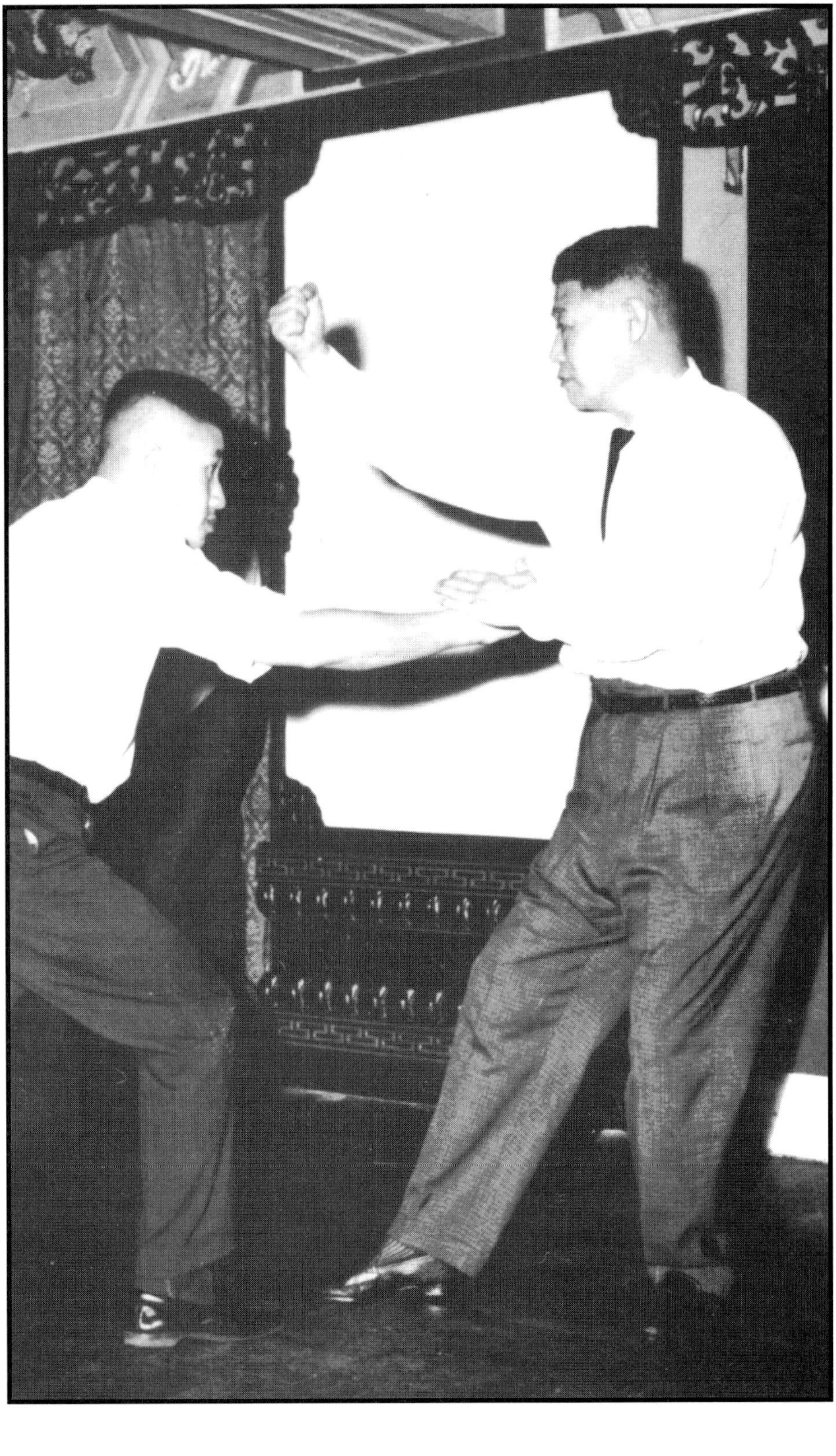

Chapter 14

楊家太極拳
老拳譜

**Yang Family
Old Manual**

Yang Family Old Manual

The first group of Tai Chi Chuan concepts :

粘 黏 連 隨

Nian, Nian, Lian, Sui
(Touch, Adhere, Link and Follow)

1. 粘   **Nian** or *Touch*:   To lift so as to uproot

2. 黏   **Nian** or *Adhere*:   To be deeply attached as if with sentiment

3. 連   **Lian** or *Link*:   To forsake oneself without losing contact or breakage

4. 隨   **Sui** or *Follow*:   To respond to the opponent's changes in movements.

The second group of Tai Chi Chuan concepts:

頂 偏 丟 抗

Ding, Pian, Diu, Kang
(Resist, Tilt, Throw and Confront)

These are all commonly made mistakes by Tai Chi practitioners.

1. 頂 **Ding** or *resist*: Taking too early the initiative to resist & to stop the opponent from advancing.

2. 偏 **Pian** or *tilt*: Insufficiency in maintaining the balance and centre.

3. 丟 **Diu** or *throw*: Losing contact through being left behind or separated without any awareness of it happening.

4. 抗 **Kang** or *confront*: Excessive use of application of moves to confront the opponent.

身形腰頂

Shen Xing Yao Ding

(The Body Shape and Usage of the Waist)

身形腰頂豈可無
缺一何必費功夫
腰頂窮研生不已
身形順我自伸舒
舍此真理終何極
十年數載亦糊塗

Translation:

Using the body and waist are the basic prerequisites of Tai Chi Chuan.

Without either, practising the art is just a waste of effort.

It takes a lifetime to understand the usage of the waist.

When one feels comfortable with the flow of the body movements,

one should feel natural and relaxed.

If one abandons this principle, one will achieve no end result.

One will still be confused even after ten or more years of practice.

太極圈

（綫香功） **Tai Chi Juan**

(Xian Xiang Gong)

Translation : Tai Chi Circle
(also known as The Coil Incense Kung)

退圈容易進圈難
不離腰頂後與前
所難中土不離位
退易進難仔細研
此為動功非站定
倚身進退並比肩
能如水磨摧急緩
雲龍風虎象周旋
要用天盤從此覓
久而久之出天然

Translation:

It is easier to leave a circle than to enter it.

The emphasis is on the hip movement whether front or back.

The difficulty is to maintain the position without shifting the centre.

To analyse and understand the above situation is to do with movement and not with a stationary posture.

Advancing and retreating by turning sideways in line with the shoulders, one is capable of turning like a millstone, fast or slow, as if whirling like a dragon in the clouds or sensing the approach of a fierce tiger.

From this, one can learn the usage of the movement of the upper torso.

Through long practice, such movement will become natural.

對待用功法守中土
Dui Dai Yong Gong Fa Shou Zhong Tu

（俗名站樁）

Translation:

Maintain the centre position in confrontation

定之方中足有根
先明四正進退身
掤攄擠按自四手
須費功夫得其真
身形腰頂皆可以
粘黏連隨意氣均
運動知覺來相應
神是君位骨肉臣
分明火候七十二
天然乃武並乃文

Translation:

To remain stable and centred, one must have good rooting at the feet.

To comprehend the four directions of movements (i.e. forward, backward, left and right), and the basic four arm movements of *Peng, Lu, Ji* and *An*, one needs much time and practice in order to appreciate the true meaning.

One should therefore be able to execute the body and waist movement.

The applications of touch, adhere, link and follow will be filled with *Yi* (intention) and *Chi*, coupled with sensitivity to respond.

The *Shen* (spirit) is the master while the bones and muscles are the servants.

There is a distinction of seventy-two different levels of standard in Tai Chi Chuan.

This also depends on the ability to mix hardness and softness.

太極膜脈筋穴解

Tai Chi Mo Mai Jin Xue Jie

The explanation of capillaries, arteries, tendons and pressure points usage in Tai Chi Chuan.

節膜拿脈抓筋閉穴
此四功由尺寸
分毫得之而後求之
膜若節之,血不週流
脈若拿之,氣難行走
筋若抓之,身無主地
穴若閉之,神昏氣暗
抓膜節之半死
申脈拿之似亡
單筋抓之勁斷
死穴閉之無生
攬之氣血精神若無
身何有主也
如能節拿抓閉之功
非得點傳不可

Translation:

To penetrate the capillaries, to hold the arteries, to grab the tendons and to block the pressure points are four skills used in Tai Chi Chuan.

Before one can apply any of these skills one must be able to determine and understand the subtlety and precise positioning of the above within the body.

If the flow of the capillaries is blocked, blood will not circulate.

If the flow of the arteries is attacked, this will disrupt the circulation of *Chi*.

If the tendons are damaged, one loses the co-ordination of the body.

When the pressure points are attacked, this will make one lifeless and dizzy and could also put one's life in danger.

To block the capillaries will cause one to be half-dead.

To attack the arteries will cause one to feel as if dying.

To damage the tendons will break one's strength and power.

To attack the "death" pressure point will result in death.

To achieve these levels of skill, true knowledge and training methods are only transmitted directly by the master to the accepted disciple/s.

太極上下名天地

Tai Chi Shan Xia Ming Tian De

The upper and lower movements of Tai Chi are the Heaven and Earth.

四手上下分天地
採挒肘靠由有去
採天靠地相應求
何患上下不既濟
若使挒肘習遠離
迷了乾坤遺歎惜
此說亦明天地盤
進用肘挒歸人字

Translation:

The four arm movements of *Peng, Lu, Ji* and *An* consist of the co-ordination of the upper and lower body i.e. heaven and earth.

The movements of *Cai, Lie, Zhou* and *Kao* also have a similar principle.

To execute *Cai* (pull) and *Kao* (shoulder) with the co-ordination of the upper and lower body, one is not concerned with not being able to release the full power.

Whereas when one uses *Lie* (split) or *Zhou* (elbow) far away from the centre, even with the co-ordination of heaven and earth, the application is still ineffective.

This demonstrates the relationship of the upper and lower parts of the body.

It also points out that the application requires training and practice so as to establish complete mastery.

Internal and External Power

勁   **Jin** or essence of power derives from the tendons.

力   **Li** or strength derives from the bones.

For example a person who can lift heavy objects demonstrates the use of external power derived from the muscles, bones, skin and hair and possesses hard physical strength. Whereas one who possesses *Jin* often seems unable to lift a few pounds in weight but is actually internally strong from spirit and *Chi*. Should one successfully acquire *Jin,* one is far superior to the one who possesses mere hard physical strength. Aiming at developing *Jin* is the correct way of exercising and reinforcing the body.

Chapter 15

Tai Chi Chuan Terminology

Tai Chi Chuan Terminology

1. ## 中定
   ### Zhong Ding *(Centred)*

The position one is in before the start of any movements such as stretching, bending, opening or closing, is referred to as the centre position or *Zhong*. When one stays in stillness this is referred to as the stable position or *Ding*. When one is calm and the mind is clear of thoughts with the spirit rising to the head, and the body is not inclining or leaning, this is known as being centred or *Zhong Ding*. It is also the basis of Taoism.

2. ## 虛領頂勁
   ### Xu Ling Ding Jin
   (Empty the crown to push up the energy)

Pushing up the energy involves the stretching and extending of the back of the neck. This is commonly referred to as *Ding Tou Xuan* (or suspending the head). The abdomen must be relaxed without any tension. The *Chi* must settle at the *Dan Tian*. The spirit rises to the crown of the head. It is like a well-centred round-based doll weighted at the bottom – light at the top and heavy at the base. When pushed at any point, it will sway and return to its upright position. It is also like a buoy floating on water, which will never sink. As the Chinese saying goes,

> " *if the essence of power is pure with the natural sinking of Chi at the Dan Tian, then flowing in harmony with the rise and fall of the waves, even when encountering a heavy storm, with a light top and weighted base, no force could turn you upside down* ".

3. 感覺
Gan Jue (*Sensitivity*)

Feeling from the body and sensing from the *Xin* (or "heart") activate one's reactions. All movement and stillness can be felt. There is always a reaction to any response. The reaction then becomes something to be felt and is a continuous process. The essence of sensitivity is very subtle and delicate. This helps one's understanding of principles and their application. The initial emphasis of push hands is to practise and train the ability to feel and sense. As one becomes responsive to touch, one can swiftly change the subtlety of the moves. This is an ongoing process.

4. 聽勁
Ting Jin (*Listening Energy*)

To listen is to measure or assess the intensity of the opponent's force. In push hands, one uses *Ting Jin* to detect the opponent's intention. One "listens" from the *Xin* (or "heart") as if one is using the ears. Initiate the flow of the *Chi* then express through the hands. Hence, use the *Xin* to initiate the *Yi* (or intention), then use *Yi* to initiate the *Chi* to circulate through the body. Listen before you react to the opponent's force. *Ting Jin* must be accurate and swift. One can then follow the opponent's movements effortlessly.

5. 問答

Wen Da *(Question and Answer)*

When a question is raised there is always an answer. Questioning and answering generates motion and stillness. When there is movement, the principle of substantial and insubstantial will be present and clearly defined. In push hands, one probes with the intention, raises the question through *Jin* and waits for the opponent's response. One then listens to where the opponent's substantial and insubstantial lie. If there is no reply, one advances and attacks. If a response is perceived, then one listens to the opponent's speed, direction and intensity before one determines where the substantial and insubstantial are.

6. 虛實

Xu Shi *(Insubstantial and Substantial)*

Presenting false information is frequently used in military tactics and one wins by using deception. This also applies to martial arts application. Deception in Tai Chi Chuan means manipulating *Xu* (insubstantial) and *Shi* (substantial). Postures, movements, applications and power generation all have different ways of using the *Xu* and *Shi* principle. To effectively apply the principle, one must have good understanding. The appearance of insubstantial is substantial and vice versa. Either use the insubstantial or the substantial in order to attack its opposite. Focus above but attack below. Sound the attention from the East but attack from the West. Approach with heaviness, then change to lightness and vice versa. The invisible and visible do not have any fixed pattern. To sink and float are indeterminable. This makes the opponent unable to detect one's *Xu* and *Shi*. Instead, one is probing the opponent's weakness all the time. Avoid the opponent's substantial and attack his insubstantial. Adapt to changes in response to opportunity. Listen to the opponent's *Jin*. Observe the movements. Seize the opportunity and attack the opponent's structure as if like a doctor who is prescribing medicine according to the ailment by questioning the symptoms, listening to the pulse, observing facial appearance etc. There is a saying:

> " One must distinguish between Xu and Shi.
> There is always Shi and Xu in any posture, and
> in any posture Shi and Xu must exist ".

7. 量敵
Liang Di (*Measure the Opponent*)

In military tactics, knowing oneself and the opponent, with a hundred battles fought, one will win a hundred battles. Hence, before setting out any logistic plan, one has to scrutinise oneself and the opponent in order to assess the probability of the outcome. In actual fact, the chances of winning or losing depend very much on knowledge or ignorance. In martial arts, although there are few philosophical terms, the principle remains. To use one's weakness against the opponent's strength is referred to as unplanned strategy. Instead, using one's strength against the opponent's weakness is good strategy and is the way of success. Between winning and losing, the importance lies in assessing or measuring the opponent's position.

The "questioning and answering" in Tai Chi Chuan is to probe the opponent's movement. The purpose is to listen to the direction and centre of his force, which will reveal the intention. This is known as *Liang Di*.

Before initiating any attack :
- *One must stay still to anticipate the opponent's movement.*
- *One should relax and let the opponent do all the hard work.*
- *Do not formulate any opinion relating to the opponent's intention.*
- *Do not guess or assume!*
- *One should not make any movement before the opponent moves, but make the move as soon as the opponent's movement is initiated.*

Hence, the essence and beauty of such skill is one's ability to detect the substantial and insubstantial and respond to it according to the opponent's changes in movement.

8. 知機

Zi Ji *(Know the Opportunity)*

Opportunity means that before the separation of *yin* and *yang*, there is nothing to conceive. Prior to the existence of opportunity, there is no sound, smell, shape or symptom. In application, there is neither motion nor stillness before the formation of shape, and thus no opportunity exists. The level of skill achieved determines your ability to recognise the availability of opportunities, thus allowing you to create and control the situation by forming something from nothing and to seize the opportunity to act. However, less skilled people will never be able to comprehend the existence of opportunity and hence will not be able to act accordingly. As a Chinese saying goes:

> *" Whoever knows first will sense first.*
> *Whoever knows last will sense last.*
> *For those who do not know,*
> *they will never be able to sense."*

This describes the three different levels of attained skills. Tai Chi Chuan practitioners will understand and know through *Tui Shou* (or push hands) the difference in levels of their abilities without having the need to compete to determine the outcome. This is almost like the Chinese game of *Go*: a master player's every move is made in accordance with a long-term strategy which allows him to dominate, and finally to decide a game. The unaccomplished player often is short sighted, without a clearly defined strategy or approach, and therefore is manipulated at all times by the master player - a sure sign of losing. Push Hands follows the same principle. The accomplished person is calm and relaxed, absorbing and neutralising whatever pressure is applied by the opponent. The less skilled individual can neither advance nor retreat from the situation. This is the difference between knowing and not knowing the opportunity.

9. 重心

Chong Xin *(Weighting)*

There are numerous postures in standing and leaning. There is a weighting created in any posture. With a correct stable posture, one is centred and is in control of the situation. Incorrect weighting will lead to the danger of falling over and losing control of the situation.

In any martial art, the applications of the forms are dependent on one's stability and correct weighting. The weighting can be in a stationary or moving posture. The stationary posture generally depends on one's practice and training in each movement of the form. One should place frequent emphasis on stability when turning, advancing or retreating. There is a correlation between the concept of weighting and substantial and insubstantial. In substantial and insubstantial, there is a constant change from emptiness to fullness, whereas weighting, though movable, dictates the stability of the body structure and therefore is rarely hastily transferred, to avoid detection by the opponent.

In combat, the *Xin* (or "heart") is the command, the *Chi* is the flag and the waist is the banner. Tai Chi Chuan uses the *Jin* as the weapon, substantial and insubstantial as strategy, the *Yi* with the *Chi* as Commander, listening or sensing as the scout and weighting as the Field Marshal. Practitioners should spend time understanding and incorporating these concepts in their training so that they can apply them fully. The activity of weighting, during contest, means that one must maintain one's centre and balance and attack the opponent's centre in order to protect the "Field Marshal" and avoid being placed in a vulnerable position.

10. 雙 重

Shuang Chong (*Double Weighting*)

Shuang Chong means without either substantial or insubstantial. The weakness of *Shuang Chong* can occur either in an individual or two people, in both hands or feet. As mentioned in the classics:

> " *Focusing on one side, one can easily follow. However, the presence of Shuang Chong leads to sluggishness*".

In addition, it is also mentioned:

> " *People have practised for a number of years and are still unable to make use of the concepts in the form due to lack of understanding of Shuang Chong*".

Therefore the weakness of *Shuang Chong* is difficult for one to detect, and is unavoidable without understanding the principles of substantial and insubstantial. Once overcome, the understanding of sensing, feeling, substantial and insubstantial, and interaction (action and response) will all be resolved. The reason why a bicycle is able to move with ease is based on principles of mechanics. The cyclist uses his hands to manoeuvre while using his feet to pedal, eyes to observe and the body to follow. The weighting is in the waist. The gears are situated in the middle of the bicycle. The motion of the bicycle is created by the up and down movement of the pedals through the use of the feet i.e. through pushing down on one while allowing the other to lift. This causes the chain on the gear to move the wheels round, thus moving the bicycle forward. If both feet were to push down at the same time, it would stop the motion of the bicycle. This is the shortcoming of *Shuang Chong*.

The same applies to push hands. When the opponent pushes and one resists with the same amount of physical force, it results in a struggle. This process becomes sluggish and is referred to as *Shuang Chong* in two people. If one party instead of resisting merges his movement with the opponent's pressure and entices him to enter into his emptiness, the process of not resisting, or letting go, will create a situation where the physical force will fall into emptiness. This is referred to as *"leaning"*.

If one intends to attack and unbalance the opponent from the side, pushing directly with both hands, one will not be able to gain any advantage if the opponent is physically stronger. In this situation, one needs to apply the principle of substantial and insubstantial, with both hands against the opponent's shoulders, using one's left hand to pull down his right shoulder and at the same time attacking his left shoulder with one's right palm. This results in both hands crossing and applying a force aiming in the same direction, forming a circular spiral, thus causing the opponent to fall sideways. This is because the opponent cannot deal with both sides, above and below at the same time, and thus loses the advantage. This is also caused by the angular projection of the force applied. Learning one concept will help practitioners to gain understanding of many other concepts. Perfecting the practice of *Shuang Chong* will lead one to a better understanding of *Dong Jin* (or interpreting energy).

11. 捨己從人

She Ji Cong Ren
(To abandon oneself, to follow the opponent)

To abandon one's own idea and to follow the opponent's movement is the most difficult task in Tai Chi Chuan. When sparring with an opponent, the mind is laden with the thought of winning or losing. Each individual is unable to bear the presence of the other. At times of attacking or struggling, it is difficult to give up one's independent action and to merge with and follow the opponent's movement. Yet this is still only a superficial explanation of what the phrase means. In Tai Chi Chuan terms, there is a far deeper meaning. The practitioner should work on the development of his personality and attitude. The classics say:

> *" The mechanics of motion and stillness are born from emptiness, the mother of Yin and Yang".*

Motion and stillness are the characteristics, *Yin* and *Yang* are the principles. Hence the theory of these characteristics and principles is the basic essence of one's self-development. The practitioner should study, nurture and develop these concepts at all times so that he fully understands and appreciates them. In time, one will attain a high level of understanding and apply these concepts with ease. From constant practice, one comes to *Dong Jin*. This will lead one to the ultimate level. This is the principle of the cyclical process - from the beginning to the ultimate and back to the beginning again. This is referred to as *"beyond the outer shell and realising the essence in the core"*. At this level, one can create situations and no longer worry about missing opportunities. When one is able to follow the bend and endure the stretch, one is unhindered and not in a disadvantaged position. This is known as *"She Ji Cong Ren"*.

12. 鼓盪

Gu Dang *(Resonating Drum)*

Sinking the *Chi*, loosening the waist, relaxing the abdomen, hollowing the chest to raise the back, sinking the shoulder to drop the elbow, extending every joint, motion and stillness, substantial and insubstantial, breathing in and out, opening and closing, hard and soft, and slow and fast. The combination of these factors gives rise to *"Gu Dang"*.

Using the *Xin* (or "heart") to direct the circulation of *Chi* through the body will give rise to the power of *Gu Dang*. Combining the mind and the *Chi* brings about changes in *Yin* and *Yang* which are like tidal waves and hurricanes, clouds drifting and the continuous flow of water, the flying albatross and fish jumping out of water, the running of rabbits and eagles preying, sinking and floating, appearing and disappearing, dramatic changes in the atmosphere and unpredictable weather.

The ultimate stage of push hands in Tai Chi Chuan is called *"the picking of flowers"*, also known as *"surfing the waves"*. This uses the *jin* of *Gu Dang* to make the opponent vibrate as if he was in a boat, trapped in a hurricane, helplessly going through the troughs and crests of the waves, rolling precariously to and fro. To cause the opponent to have difficulties in comprehending and anticipating one's intention is the main function of *Gu Dang*.

13. 基礎
Ji Chu *(The Fundamentals)*

Tai Chi Chuan uses the form as the structure and push hands as the application. For beginners the basic framework of the form structure is very important. The posture must be correct such that it is centred, upright and precise, natural and with extension. Movement must be gradual and even, smooth and flowing, and should be *light, nimble, whole and alive*. This is the only correct path for any practitioner in order to progress in his training without wasting time and effort.

A) 中 Zhong *(Centre)*

The mind is calm, the spirit is clear and the energy sinks. Rooting is at the feet and is the point of equilibrium. The gravity is around the waist and the spine. This is known as *"the command from the mind begins at the waist"*. The spirit is hidden within, without external sign, and will lead to centring, calmness and sinking.

B) 正 Zheng *(Upright and precise)*

Every posture is upright and accurate, avoiding leaning or tilting. In any posture, whether stretching, bending or pulling, it all depends on gravity, leading to centring, thus enabling the application and projection of *Chi*. Gravity is the main control of the body. If it is stable, one will be able to perform the posture, and "open and close" with natural ease. If it is not, the connection between open and close will be missing. This is like the shaft as the main controller of the wheels. If the shaft is misaligned, the centre of gravity will not be stable, thus losing the function of the wheels. The framework of the posture must be centred and balanced, hence enabling one to distinguish substantial and insubstantial.

C) 安 An *(Natural)*

The state of naturalness should be without any strain. One then becomes relaxed and this enables the energy to circulate in the body without any hindrance. This all comes from stable posture, even and balanced movement, natural breathing and calmness.

D) 舒 Shu *(Extension)*

There is a saying:

> *"First acquire expansion, leading to being compact and well knitted later".*

At beginner's level, the postures and movements require a large structure to allow the joints to open up. This is not done by stretching the tendons, sinews and bones intentionally. Continuous practice of the process of this natural extension and expanding will bring about the loosening of the joints and lead to sinking.

E) 輕 Qing *(Lightness)*

Qing means light and empty but not floating. When practising, the movements must be light, agile and smooth. Thus, one is able to move forward and backward with artless ease. Continuous practice will lead to a lively and "loose" strength and eventually yield the power of touching and adhering. This helps one gain insight into the basic understanding of Tai Chi Chuan softness.

F) 靈 Ling *(Nimble)*

From lightness and insubstantial to loosening and sinking, and from loosening and sinking to touching and adhering. To touch and adhere means one is able to link and follow. When one is able to link and follow, one becomes agile and understands the meaning of not confronting, and of disengaging when necessary.

G) 圓 Yuan *(Wholeness)*

The concept of *Yuan* means fullness and completeness. Every posture and movement must be completed without any flaws and be in unison. This avoids the defects of gap, breakage or unevenness. When using energy during push hands, if the mind and body are not in unison, it will not work. The ability to execute wholeness will lead to unhindered action.

H) 活 Huo *(Spry)*

This means spry and agile. No heaviness and no sluggishness. When all the above-mentioned have been assimilated, stretching, bending and closing, forward, backward, up and down, all come freely and naturally. This is what is meant by:

> *"The ability to breathe with ease will lead to spryness and agility"*.

I) 授受 Shou Shou *(Teaching and Receiving)*

Each individual has different combinations of these characteristics. *Shou Shou* can be divided into two aspects i.e. gentle or headstrong. Those who are headstrong usually rush and are fierce when they attack. The intelligent will become strong. The less intelligent will become short tempered. The strong like to compete, and in training, they tend to be physical and unable to accept losing. The gentle tend to be agreeable. The intelligent are calm and polite. When learning, they tend to put emphasis more on softness because they prefer peace and harmony. Short-tempered persons tend to be erratic. When learning they like to be fierce and have no interest in refinement of their training. The less intelligent of the gentle ones will be weak in their determination and not as motivated. When learning they do not seek to understand.

For martial arts practitioners, it is essential to have a strong will, a firm character, intelligence, kindness and courage, in order to process the quality of both power and gentleness, to enable one to enhance one's training. Each practitioner has elements of all of these and because of this, everyone has different levels of achievement. It has been observed that practitioners learning from the same teacher may have differences in understanding both the theory and practice of Tai Chi Chuan. This causes a lot of confusion and queries. In addition, these differences can also be attributed to the ways in which the teacher wishes to impart his knowledge and skills to his students based on their character and standards.

True transmission of the art is only passed down to selected disciples of the master. Hence, readers can now observe and understand the reason behind the presence of variations in Tai Chi Chuan. Students should seek out a master who has received true transmission to ensure that they will learn authentic Tai Chi Chuan. Otherwise, they will have great difficulty in understanding and achieving high levels in Tai Chi Chuan. As the Chinese say:

差之毫釐，繆以千里

" Miss by an inch, miss by a thousand miles ".

此掌與人大不同
手未動兮胯先先攻
未從前伸先後縮
吸足再吐力獨豐

Calligraphy written by Grandmaster Ip

Chapter 16

太極拳

結論

Conclusion

In *Wu Shu* (Martial Arts), the ability to alternate extreme hardness with extreme softness is regarded as the highest level of achievement. Masters of internal martial arts have the unique ability to interchange and blend these qualities - softness to hardness, no softness with no hardness, or softness with hardness. When confronted by an enemy, one takes advantage of every available opportunity and changes infinitely. When making contact, the hands appear to be soft and yet are hard, like a hammer or iron bar wrapped in cotton. One may appear vacant but when in motion, one moves with the speed and nimbleness of a monkey. Confronting such a level of skill, the enemy finds himself getting injured or thrown without ever realising what has happened. It is like a dragon flying across the sky without being detected, which signifies that the level of skill is beyond comprehension. The mastering of interchanges of softness and hardness cannot be achieved overnight and requires a long period of dedicated training.

Tai Chi Chuan is the best method of training softness as hardness. To achieve this :

- *First one must concentrate on softness and let the whole body loosen up when practising the Tai Chi Chuan form, in particular, paying attention to the upper torso and the hands.*
- *There should be no physical strength in the body and arms, as if they were an empty shell.*
- *The focus is all on the lower body i.e. waist and legs.*

In time, one slowly replaces physical strength with a new type of internal strength. With *Chi* energy sunk in the *Dan Tian* and the spirit rising to the crown, one benefits boundlessly. This leads to the highest technique of combining softness and hardness.

Tai Chi Chuan is an exercise using the mind to direct the *Yi* and the

Conclusion

circulation of energy, and to increase the flexibility of the body. Using *Yi,* not physical strength, with daily practice allows the circulation of *Chi* through the body, and one will acquire genuine internal energy through a long and consistent period of training. As the classic states:

極柔軟然後
能極堅剛也

" Extreme softness can then become extreme hardness".

April 2001: Master Ding and his students celebrating Grandmaster Ip's seventy-second birthday with his daughter, Mabel and some of his senior students.

Appendix 1

Profile of a Master

Grandmaster Ip Tai Tak

Interview conducted by Master Ding, and originally published in Tai Chi & Alternative Health magazine Volume 1, Issue 4, Spring 1995

Master Ding (MD) : Were there differences in the Yang Style Tai Chi form when you began to train under Master Yang?

Grandmaster Ip (GMI): Previous to learning under Master Yang it was very obvious that there were differences in my Yang Style Tai Chi form. As a result of this I had to relearn the whole form. Master Yang's movements were simpler to the eye, yet had focused precision to match. Even though the movements seemed simplistic, the traditional form was more difficult to master as it involved many intricate subtleties needing only very small movements, which are hardly noticeable to the eye. When he was correcting me, Master Yang often told me that he was screwing my structure down. In other words he was reinforcing the structure so that it could enable the *Chi* power to be more concentrated and thus more projected. Practising the corrected form brings quicker results.

Master Yang also said that if the form's postures and movements were not correct, whatever time and energy is put into the practice, the effort is wasted. It can be likened to pouring water into a bucket full of holes. Water cannot be retained in the bucket, so therefore time and energy put into filling the bucket can never yield the desired results. Practising the correct form ensures that the time and effort put into the practice is not wasted. Each practice session helps to concentrate and harness the power a little more i.e. the bucket without holes can retain water without loss each time it is filled a little.

MD : What other differences are there?

GMI: The traditional Yang Form has more meaning and enables me to cultivate more power quicker. The *Chi* energy is more focused and direct, hence more effective for self-defence application. The form uses numerous circular movements within various postures through the use of hip movements. The previous form that I had learnt had no depth or meaning. Correct weighting is also very important. Practitioners should ensure that the weighting within the forward postures should always be 70/30 (70% of the weighting on the front leg and 30% on the rear leg) and should never be double-weighted i.e. 50/50.

I have also observed that a number of Yang Style forms are often too relaxed and flowery. Traditional Yang style postures are simple and yet contain various subtleties incorporated within them. Practitioners should always seek out a Master who can demonstrate and show such levels of teachings. Without it, people often get stuck at their levels and are unable to progress any further in Tai Chi Chuan training. It is common to find these people giving up Tai Chi or using an external martial arts approach to explain the principles and applications of Tai Chi Chuan. The latter approach usually leads the practitioner further and further away from gaining insight and understanding of the true meaning of *Internal Martial Arts*.

MD: What was the training like under Master Yang?

GMI: Master Yang was a traditionalist. He taught on an individual basis and expected high standards from all his students. The training was very tough indeed! I often remember having to change T-shirts during my training sessions for they were always drenched with sweat. Master Yang would sometimes tell me that people nowadays generally do not train very hard when compared with his own or previous generations' training. For instance, Master Yang's father, Yang Cheng Fu, often woke him early in the mornings, even in the very cold winter, insistent that he should train in the courtyard. Without training, Master Yang was not allowed back into the house. During bitter cold winters in China, to survive, young Master Yang had to train in the courtyard in fear of freezing to death. He would practice his form over and over again just to keep himself warm. Only after diligent practice was he allowed back into the house to have breakfast. Master Yang often said that his father would practise intensively in a cycle until he was completely exhausted. After an intensive session his father slept only by lying on a thin board rested at an angle on the wall. By doing this, should he sleep too comfortably, and roll over, he would fall off the board (thereby waking himself), wash his face with cold water and resume training again. This cycle was continuous so that he trained intensively 24 hours a day.

MD: What are the essential points when practising Tai Chi Chuan?

GMI: There are three important aspects of training that one has to take into consideration to improve one's Tai Chi Chuan:

a. Correct practice of the form – this will enable one to circulate *Chi* energy and also gain better understanding of its applicability.

b. *Zhan Zhong Chi Kung* training. This form of training not only helps practitioners to focus and harness *Chi* but also strengthens one's stability and balance.

c. Push Hands. This enables one to develop one's sensitivity and *Ting Jin* (or listening energy) for self-defence applications.

If the individual carries out these three important approaches in training, his Tai Chi Chuan will progress much more quickly to a higher level.

Appendix 1

MD: What advice would you give to individuals who want to improve their Tai Chi Chuan?

GMI: The individual should seek out a reputable, skilled and knowledgeable Master. The attitude and approach of the student is also very important. In ancient times, before an individual was accepted to undertake training, his character was assessed. This assessment would continue throughout his training from the initial to advanced stages. Failing such testing meant that the student would no longer be allowed to study the art further. Constant and regular practice is vital. Results in one's training are measured in ten-year periods. To be good in Tai Chi Chuan, you have to be committed and able to endure hard training. Correct postures are important. These are the building blocks for strong foundation. Bad postures give rise to poor foundation and further training will yield little gain.

MD: Often I hear people say that if they are intelligent they could learn the form quicker and are able to achieve high levels in Tai Chi Chuan more easily. What is your view about this?

GMI: The training in Tai Chi Chuan is quite different from ordinary academic studies. The individual will still need to practise to gain better understanding of the form. In Chinese, we often use the millstone to explain the concept of correct form practice. For example, wheat grains are put in the mill to be turned into flour, which can then be used for numerous purposes. Form practising is similar in that over a period of time of continued practice you will gain better understanding and insight into different aspects and applications of *Chi* within the form. Some intelligent people often ask the Master to teach more postures at each session so they can memorise and remember more moves. However, each correct posture needs to be practised regularly before learning new moves otherwise the full essence of the postures is not grasped. Time spent learning a few postures correctly at each session is more valuable and important than learning many postures incorrectly.

MD: Some practitioners often try to learn from different Masters who are conducting various workshops or seminars. Will they be able to learn much Tai Chi to improve their levels?

GMI: People attending such workshops or seminars do gain some understanding of the different approaches of Tai Chi Chuan as demonstrated by these Masters. People generally learn numerous forms, pushing hands, weapons, etc. These are merely movements and often taught only at basic levels. To achieve high levels in Tai Chi Chuan, you should seek out the best and continue to study with that Master. Higher levels or skills are normally only taught to people who have stayed with the Master for long periods of time. The time factor is not the only determinant. Your character and personality are also taken into account because the Master needs to feel that the individual is worthy of the true transmission. Hence, you can see why a Master teaching thousands of students may only have a handful of disciples. The late Master Yang Sau Chung only accepted three disciples – myself, Chu Gin Soon and Chu King Hung.

MD: Practitioners often get asked what family style of Tai Chi Chuan they practised and whether they are big or small circle? Could you explain what they mean?

GMI: Big or small circle often means that the form is practised with larger or smaller circular movements (for example Wu Style is said to be small circle). However, other than this framework, the less known versions of the Yang Style form are classified into three types - *stork, tiger* and *snake*.

Stork – the postures in the form tend to be much higher. This form is ideal for weaker or older people to practise.

Tiger – the postures are of medium height and should be aimed at by all practitioners.

Snake – the postures are very low. This is the most difficult form to master. Only the inner disciples are taught this higher level. This form is not suitable for everybody to practise. We hear stories of different generations of Yang Masters who develop such flexibility and dexterity that they are able to practise the form under table tops and even pick up coins from the ground with their mouth while in "snake creeps down" posture. Practitioners should not attempt to practice this snake form without the supervision and instruction of a knowledgeable and experienced Tai Chi Master.

MD: We often hear stories of the Yang Masters' power and applications for self-defence. What was training under Master Yang Sau Chung like in this respect?

GMI: My Master often stated that to understand *Chi* energy and its self-defence application, one needs to experience being attacked or hit by the Master. He often stressed that if he did not hit or attack the student, they would not understand nor learn the true internal concept of self-defence. In Chinese (Cantonese), this process is called:

"BUT DA BUT GAU"

or "Not to hit, is not to teach".

For instance, to cook a dish, you first need to know the right ingredients. To taste such a dish, one needs to use the senses of touch, smell, sight and taste, to really appreciate the true flavour of the dish. Therefore, the only way to understand is to experience. In the past, when these Yang Masters taught their students, they had to endure very harsh and tough training. Some of these students often got injured or gave up studying Tai Chi altogether, as they could not endure such rigorous training.

I have personally undergone 34 years of this type of training. Initially, when I practised advanced pushing hands with my Master, as soon as I had contact with him, I was immediately thrown to the wall. Often when pushed, I would bounce off the wall like a ball. During the earlier stages of my training, I often saw "stars" and got very breathless. Over a period of time, through such regular practice, I became stronger. Depending on the intensity of *Chi* energy applied by my Master, I was able to cope with the force to some degree by feeling and reacting to it –something that can only be learnt through such conditioning and experience. Master Yang could use any part of his body to apply his *Chi* energy, for example in *Fa Jin* (or issuing energy). In my training session, I was usually exhausted and drenched in sweat after practising advanced pushing hands with Master Yang. However, he still appeared as fresh as when he first started the session. Not even a drop of sweat! He was always able to control the *Chi* with such precision and focus at all times, using minimal or no movement at all. His power was indescribable and had to be felt to be appreciated.

MD: What other aspects of training would you give to Tai Chi Chuan practitioners to help them improve their standards?

GMI: People need to be aware of three other principles:

Appendix 1

a. **Yuen** *(or circular)* -Tai Chi Chuan movements are usually circular. However, within this circular nature, the shape could change, for instance, smaller and large circles, oblong and so on.

b. **Wan** *(or smooth flow)* – movements practised need to be smooth and in flowing momentum. There should not be a break from the beginning to the end i.e. like the *Yin –Yang* symbol, one flowing into the other.

c. **Tuen** *(or united)* – the movement practised should be co-ordinated and balanced.

MD: I would like to thank you for this rare interview. I am sure that I have gained a more expansive view of Tai Chi Chuan and that readers will undoubtedly gain a valuable insight into Tai Chi Chuan.

Thank you

Profile of a Master

發勁送後退
鼓尾腰進
命閂頂並
門彈倚比
前簽身肩

Calligraphy written by Grandmaster Ip

Appendix 2

Traditional Yang Style Tai Chi Chuan Form Posture List

First Part

Chinese (Pu Tung Hua)

1. Preparation
   a. Feet Together with Both Hand on Sides of Body
2. Beginning
   a. Right Foot Apart with Hands on the Sides
   b. Lift and Lower Hands
   c. Tai Chi Circle Hands
3. Grasp the Bird's Tail
   a. Shift Weight to Right Foot and Hold the Ball
   b. Single Ward Off (Left)
   c. Double Ward Off
   d. Pull Down (Left)
   e. Press
   f. Push
   g. Sit Back and Push to the Left
   h. Sit Back and Push to the Right
4. Single Whip
5. Lift Hands
   a. Pull Down (Left)
   b. Elbow / Shoulder Strike
   c. Ward Off (Right)
6. White Crane Spreads Its Wings
7. Left Brush Knee and Push
8. Hands Strumming Pi Pa
9. Left Brush Knee and Push
10. Right Brush Knee and Push
11. Left Brush Knee and Push
12. Hands Strumming Pi Pa
13. Left Brush Knee and Push
    a. Right Hand Forms Fist, Bring it Down to the Left
14. Step Forward - Parry and Punch
15. Apparent Seal Off
16. Crossing Hands

1. Yu Bei Sai

2. Tai Chi Che Shih

3. Lan Chiao Wei
   a. Her Shou
   b. Zuo Peng
   c. You Peng
   d. Lu
   e. Ji
   f. An
   g. Zuo Tui
   h. You Tui
4. Tan Pien
5. Ti Shou Shang Shih
   a. Lui
   b. Zhou / Kao
   c. Peng
6. Pai Hao Liang Che
7. Zuo Lou Hsih Au Bu
8. Shou Hui Pi Pa
9. Zuo Lou Hsih Au Bu
10. You Lou Hsih Au Bu
11. Zuo Lou Shih Au Bu
12. Shou Hui Pi Pa
13. Zuo Lou Hish Au Bu

14. Chin Pu Pan Lan Chui
15. Yue Fung Shih Pi
16. Shih Tzu Shao

Appendix 2

Second Part

17. Embrace Tiger Return to Mountain
18. Grasp the Bird's Tail
    a. *Bring Right Hand Up*
    b. *Pull Down (Left)*
    c. *Press*
    d. *Push*
    e. *Sit Back and Push to the Left*
    f. *Sit Back and Push to the Right*
    g. *Lift Arms, Turn and Block to the Left*
    h. *Push Straight Forward (Left Diagonal Direction)*
19. Fist Under Elbow
20. Back Stepping Monkey (Right)
21. Back Stepping Monkey (Left)
22. Back Stepping Monkey (Right)
23. Back Stepping Monkey (Left)
24. Back Stepping Monkey (Right)
25. Diagonal Flying (Right)
26. Lift Hands
    a. *Pull Down (Left)*
    b. *Elbow/Shoulder Strike*
    c. *Ward Off (Right)*
27. White Crane Spreads Its Wings
28. Left Brush Knee and Push (Right)
29. Needle at Sea Bottom
30. Fan Through Back
31. Turn Body and Punch
    a. *Punch Up and Pull Down*
32. Step Forward, Parry and Punch
    a. *Sit Back and Pull Down (Right)*
33. Left Diagonal Flying
34. Step Forward Grasp the Bird's Tail
    a. *Double Ward Off*
    b. *Pull Down (Left)*

17. *Pao Hu Kwei Shan*
18. *Lan Chiao Wei*
    a. *Ti You Shou*
    b. *Lu*
    c. *Ji*
    d. *An*
    e. *Zuo Tui*
    f. *You Tui*
    g.

    h.

19. *Chou Te Chui*
20. *You Tao Nien Hou*
21. *Zuo Tao Nien Hou*
22. *You Tao Nien Hou*
23. *Zuo Tao Nien Hou*
24. *You Tao Nien Hou*
25. *Hsia Fei Shih*
26. *Ti Shou Shang Shih*
    a. *Lu*
    b. *Zhou / Kao*
    c. *You Peng*
27. *Pai Hao Liang Che*
28. *Zuo Lou Hsih Au Pu*
29. *Hai Te Chen*
30. *Shan Tung Pei*
31. *Chuan Shen Pi Shen Chui*

32.. *Chin Bu Pan Lan Chui*

33. *Hsia Fei Shih*
34. *Lan Chiao Wei*
    a. *Peng*

  c. Press
  d. Push
  e. Sit Back and Push to the Left
  f. Sit Back and Push to the Right
35. Single Whip
36. Cloud Hands
  a. Repeat Cloud Hands - 5 Times on the
   Left Side and 4 Times on the Right Side
   and Ending on the Right Side
37. Single Whip
38. High Pat on Horse
39. Separate and Kick Right
40. Separate and Kick Left
41. Turn and Kick with Heel (Left)
42. Left Brush Knee and Push
43. Right Brush Knee and Push
44. Step Forward and Punch Down
45. Turn Body and Punch
  a. Punch Up and Pull Down
46. Step Forward, Parry and Punch
47. Left Diagonal Flying
48. Kick with Right Heel
  a. Push to the Right
49. Strike Tiger Left
50. Strike Tiger Right
51. Block with Left Arm and Kick with
  Right Heel
52. Double Phoenix Attacking the Ears
53. Kick with Left Heel
54. Turn Body and Kick with Right Heel
  a. Left Pull Down
55. Step Forward, Parry and Punch
56. Apparent Seal Off
57. Crossing Hands

  b. Zuo Lu
  c. Ji
  d. An
  e. Zuo Tui
  f. You Tui
35. Tan Pien
36. Yun Shou

37. Tan Pien
38. Kao Tan Ma
39. You Fun Chiao
40. Zuo Fun Chiao
41. Chuan Shen Tso Teng Chiao
42. Zuo Lou Hish Au Pu
43. You Lou Hsih Au Pu
44. Chin Pu Tsai Chui
45. Chuan Shen Pi Shen Chui

46. Chin Pu Pan Lan Chui
47. Zuo Hsia Fei Shih
48. You Teng Chiao

49. Zuo Da Hu
50. You Da Hu
51. Wui Shen Yu Teng Chiao

52. Shuang Fung Kuan Er
53. Zuo Teng Chiao
54. Chuan Shen Yu Teng Chiao

55. Chin Pu Pan Lan Chui
56. Yue Fung Shih Pi
57. Shih Tze Shou

Appendix 2

Third Part

58. Embrace Tiger Return to Mountain
59. Grasp the Bird's Tail
    a. Bring Right Hand Up
    b. Pull Down (Left)
    c. Press
    d. Push
    e. Sit Back and Push to the Left
    f. Sit Back and Push to the Right
60. Diagonal Single Whip
61. Parting Horse's Mane (Right)
62. Parting Horse's Mane (Left)
63. Parting Horse's Mane (Right)
    a. Turn Left and Circle Right Arm Forward
64. Grasp the Bird's Tail
    a. Ward Off (Left)
    b. Double Ward Off
    c. Pull Down (Left)
    d. Press
    e. Push
    f. Sit Back and Push to the Left
    g. Sit Back and Push to the Right
65. Single Whip
66. Lady Threads Shuttles (Left)
67. Lady Threads Shuttles (Right)
68. Lady Threads Shuttles (Left)
69. Lady Threads Shuttles (Right)
    a. Circle Left and Pull Down (Right)
70. Grasp the Bird's Tail
    a. Ward Off (Left)
    b. Double Ward Off
    c. Pull Down (Left)
    d. Press
    e. Push
    f. Sit Back and Push to the Left
    g. Sit Back and Push to the Right

58. Pao Hu Kwei Shan
59. Lan Chiao Wei
    a. Ti You Shou
    b. Lu
    c. Ji
    d. An
    e. Zuo Tui
    f. You Tui
60. Hsia Tan Pien
61. You Yeh Ma Fung Tsung
62. Zuo Yeh Ma Fung Tsung
63. You Yeh Ma Fung Tsung

64. Lan Chiao Wei
    a. Zuo Peng
    b. Shuang Peng
    c. Lu
    d. Ji
    e. An
    f. Zuo Tui
    g. You Tui
65. Tan Pien
66. Zuo Yu Nu Chuen Shu
67. You Yu Nu Chuen Shu
68. Zuo Yu Nu Chuen Shu
69. You Yu Nu Chuen Shu

70. Lan Chiao Wei
    a. Zuo Peng
    b. You Peng
    c. Lu
    d. Ji
    e. An
    f. Zuo Tui
    g. You Tui

71. Single Whip
72. Cloud Hands
   a. Repeat Cloud Hands - 4 Times Left Side and 3 Times Right Side. Ending on the Right
73. Single Whip
74. Snake Creeps Down
75. Left Golden Rooster Stands on One Leg
76. Right Golden Rooster Stands on One Leg
77. Back Stepping Monkey (Right)
78. Back Stepping Monkey (Left)
79. Back Stepping Monkey (Right)
80. Diagonal Flying (Right)
81. Lift Hands
   a. Pull Down (Left)
   b. Elbow/Shoulder Strike
   c. Ward Off Right
82. White Crane Spread Its Wings
83. Left Brush Knee and Push
84. Needle at Sea Bottom
85. Fan Through Back
86. Turn Body and Punch
   a. Punch Up and Pull Down
87. Step Forward Parry and Punch
   a. Sit Back and Pull Down (Right)
88. Left Diagonal Flying
89. Step Forward to Grasp the Bird's Tail
   a. Double Ward Off
   b. Pull Down (Left)
   c. Press
   d. Push
   e. Sit Back and Push to the Left
   f. Sit Back and Push to the Right
90. Single Whip
91. Cloud Hands
   a. Repeat 3 Times on the Left Side and

71. Tan Pien
72. Yun Shou

73. Tan Pien
74. Tan Pien Hsia Shih
75. You Chin Chi Tu Li
76. Zuo Chin Chi Tu Li
77. Zuo Tao Nien Hou
78. You Tao Nien Hou
79. Zuo Tap Nien Hou
80. Hsia Fei Shih
81. Ti Shou Shang Shih
   a. Lu
   b. Kao / Zhou
   c. You Peng
82. Pai Hao Liang Che
83. Zuo Lou Hsih Au Pu
84. Hai Te Chen
85. Shan Tung Pei
86. Chuan Shen Pi San Chui

87. Chin Pu Pan Lan Chui

88. Zuo Hsia Fei Shih
89. Chin Pu Lan Chiao Wei
   a. Shuang Peng
   b. Lu
   c. Ji
   d. An
   e. Zuo Tui
   f. You Tui
90. Tan Pien
91. Yun Shou

Third Part continued .....

2 Times on the Right. Ending on the Right.

92. Single Whip	92. Tan Pien
93. High Pat on Horse	93. Kao Tan Ma
94. Thrusting Hand	94. Chuen Chwang
95. Turn Body and Kick with Right Heel	95. Chuan Shen Yu Teng Chiao .
a. Shift Forward and Press Down	
96. Step Forward and Punch to the Groin	96. Chin Pu ChiTang Chui
a. Sit Back and Pull Down (Right)	
97. Left Diagonal Flying	97. Zuo Hsia Fei Shih
98. Step Forward To Grasp The Bird's Tail	98. Chin Pu Lan Chiao Wei
a. Double Ward Off	a. Shuang Peng
b. Pull Down (Left)	b. Lu
c. Press	c. Ji
d. Push	d. An
e. Sit Back and Push to the Left	e. Zuo Tui
f. Sit Back and Push to the Right	f. You Tui
99. Single Whip	99. Tan Pien
100. Snake Creeps Down	100. Tan Pien Hsia Shih
101. Step Up to Seven Stars	101. Shang Pu Chi Hsing
102. Step Back to Ride Tiger	102. Tui Pu Kua Hu
103. Turn Body to Sweep Lotus	103. Chuan Shen Pai Lien
104. Bend Bow to Shoot Tiger	104. Wan Kung She Hu
a. Pull Down (Left)	
105. Step Forward – Parry and Punch	105. Chin Pu Pan Lan Chui
106. Apparent Close Up and Push	106. Yue Fung Shih Pi
107. Crossing Hands	107. Shih Tze Shou
108. Conclusion	108. Kar Tai Chi Shih

Right:
Grandmaster Ip demonstrates
"Hai Te Chen" Tai Chi Chuan posture

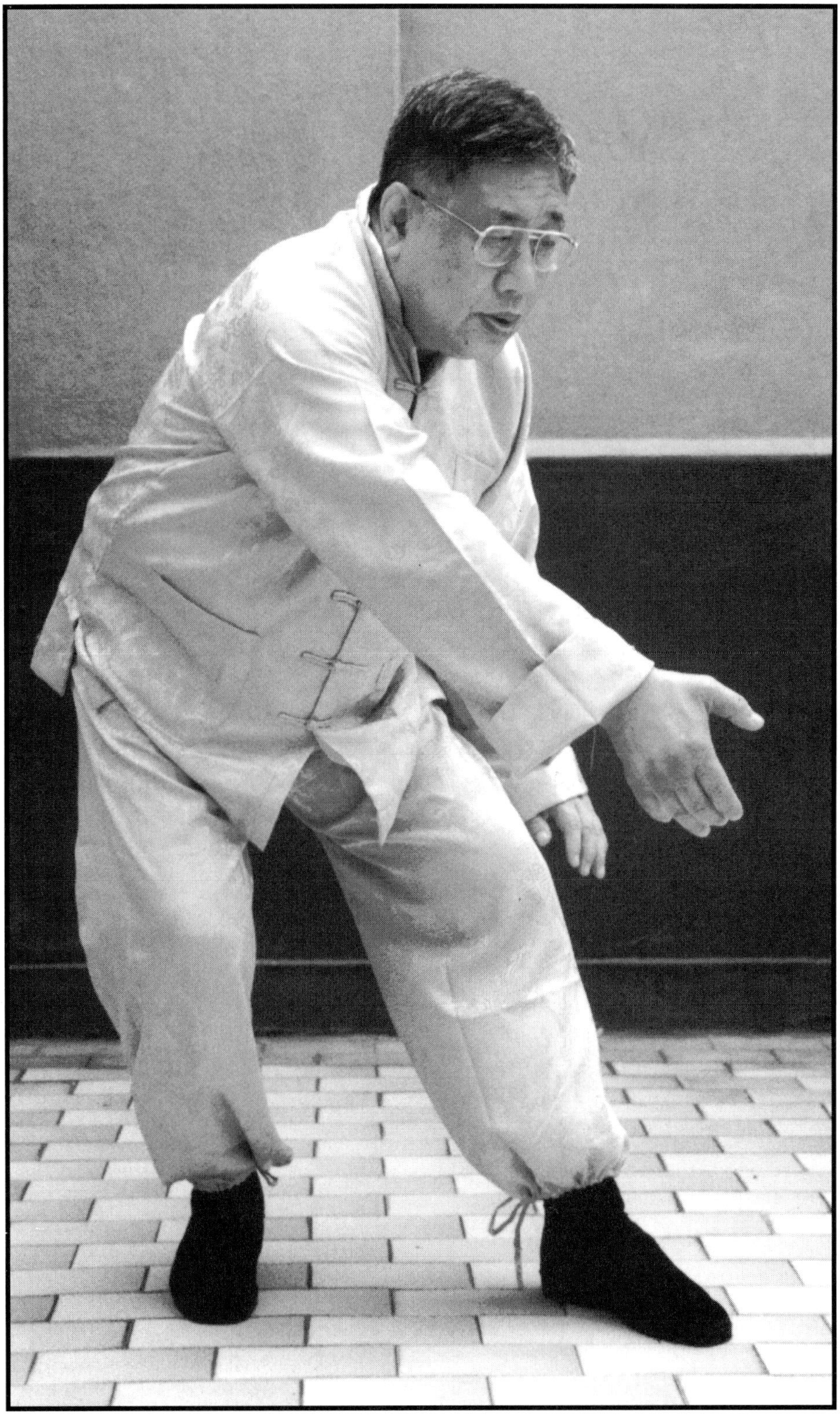

Appendix 3

Traditional Yang Style Tai Chi Sword Form

劍

Traditional Yang Style Tai Chi Sword

1. Preparation	*1. Yu Bei Shih*
2. Beginning Form	*2. Jian Che Shih*
3. Three Rings Encircle the Moon	*3. San Huan Tao Yue*
4. The Immortal Points the Way	*4. Seen Ren Yan Zi Lu*
5. The Big Dipper	*5. Da Kui Xing*
6. Swallow Draws the Water	*6. Yanzi Chao Shui*
7. Intercept and Sweep - Left and Right	*7. Zuo You Lan Sao*
8. The Little Dipper	*8. Xiao Kui Xing*
9. Swallow Enters the Nest	*9. Yanzi Ru Chao*
10. Agile Cat Catches the Mouse	*10. Ling Mao Bu Shu*
11. Dragonfly Touches the Water	*11. Qingting Dian Shui*
12. Phoenix Lifts its Head	*12. Fenghuang Ti Tou*
13. Left Whirlwind	*13. Zuo Xuanfeng*
14. Wasp Enters the Cave	*14. Huangfeng Ru Dong*
15. Phoenix Spreads its Wings	*15. Fenghuang Zhan Chi*
16. The Little Dipper	*16. Xiao Kui Xing*
17. Waiting for Fish	*17. Deng Yu Shi*
18. Moving Dragon Posture	*18. Long Hang Shih*
19. Embrace the Moon	*19. Huai Zhong Bao Yue*
20. Birds Returns to Roost in the Forest	*20. Xiu Niao Tou Lin*
21. Black Dragon Wags its Tail	*21. Wu Long Bai Wei*
22. Green Dragon Emerges from Water	*22. Qing Long Chu Shui*
23. Wind Rolls Up the Lotus Leaf	*23. Feng Juan He She*
24. Lion Shakes its Head	*24. Shizi Yao Tou*
25. Tiger Holds its Head	*25. Hu Bao Tou*
26. Wild Horse Leaps the Stream	*26. Ye Ma Tiao Jian*
27. Turn Round and Rein in the Horse	*27. Fan Shen Le Ma*

Traiditional Yang Style Tai Chi Sword continued ..

28. Compass Needle	28. Zhinan Zhen
29. Face the Wind to Dust	29. Ying Feng Fu Chen
30. Follow the Current to Push the Boat	30. Shun Shui Tui Zhou
31. Meteor Pursues the Moon	31. Liu Xing Gan Yue
32. Pegasus Gallops in the Sky	32. Tian Ma Xing Kong
33. Roll Up the Curtain	33. Tiao Lian Shih
34. Bend Down to Lower the Sword	34. Wan Shen Chui Jian
35. Cartwheel Sword – Left and Right	35. Zuo You Chelun Jian
36. Swallow Holds Mud in Mouth	36. Yanzi Xian Ni
37. Great Roc Spreads Winds	37. Da Peng Zhan Chi
38. Scoop the Moon from Bottom of Sea	38. Hai Di Lao Yue
38. Embrace the Moon	39. Huai Zhing Bao Yue
39. Na Cha Sounding the Sea	40. Na Cha Tan Hai
40. Rhinoceros Gazes at the Moon	40. Xiniu Wang Yue
41. Shoot the Wild Goose	41. She Yan Shih
42. Green Dragon Reveals Claws	42. Qing Long Xian Zhao
43. Phoenix Spreads Wings	43. Fenghuang Zhan Xue
44. Intercept – Left and Right	44. Zuo You Kua Lan
45. Shoot the Wild Goose	45. She Yan Shih
46. White Ape Offers Fruits	46. Bai Yuan Xian Guo
47. Left and Right Falling Flowers	47. Zuo You Luo Hua
48. Jade Maiden Threads the Shuttle	48. Yu Nu Chuen Shu
49. White Tiger Cocks the Tail	49. Bai Hu Jiao Wei
50. Carp Leaps Over Dragon Gate	50. Li Yue Long Men
51. Black Dragon Curls Round Pillar	51. Wu Long Jiao Zhu
52. Immortal Points the Way	52. Xian Ren Zhi Ru
53. Incense Points Toward the Sky	53. Zhao Tian Yi Zhu Xiang
54. Wind Sweeps the Plum Flower	54. Feng Sao Mei Hua
55. Hold the Ivory Tablet	55. Ya Hu Shih
56. Return Sword to Original Position	56. Bao Jian Gui Yuan

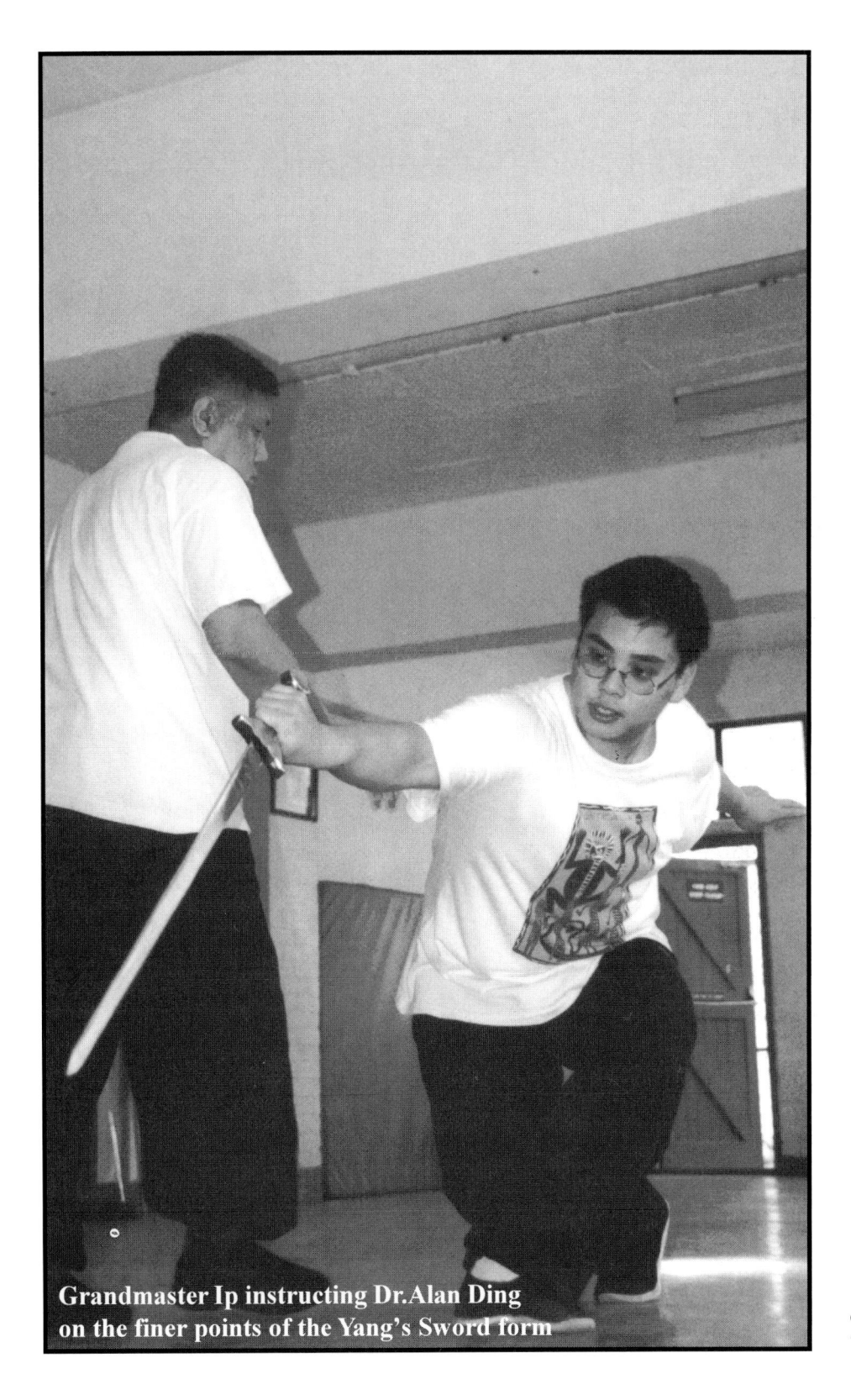

Grandmaster Ip instructing Dr. Alan Ding
on the finer points of the Yang's Sword form

Appendix 4

Traditional Yang Style Sabre Form

刀

Traditonal Yang Style Sabre Form

1. Beginning	*1. Chi Shih*
2. Step Forward to Seven Star	*2. Shang Bu Qi Xing*
3. Step Back to Ride Tiger	*3. Tui Bu Kua Hu*
4. Step Forward to Transfer Sabre	*4. Shang Bu Jiao Dao*
5. Side Step to Unfold Stabbing	*5. Shan Bu Zhan Qi*
6. Push Sabre Left and Right	*6. Zuo You Tui Dao*
7. Curling Sabre Round with Penetrating Palm	*7. Liao Dao Chuan Zhang*
8. Chang'e Maiden Heading to the Moon	*8. Chang'e Ben Yue*
9. Jade Maiden Casting Shuttle	*9. Yu Nu Pao Suo*
10. Conceal Sabre to Present Palm	*10. Zang Dao Xian Zhang*
11. Jade Maiden Casting Shuttle	*11. Yu Nu Pao Suo*
12. Conceal Sabre to Present Palm	*12. Zang Dao Xian Zhang*
13. Turn Round to Sever	*13. Fan Shen Jie Ge*
14. Raise Foot and Stab	*14. Di Jiao Ci*
15. Conceal Sabre	*15. Zang Dao Shih*
16. Step Aside and Thrust Upwards	*16. Yi Bu Shang Ci*
17. Conceal Sabre to Present Palm	*17. Zang Dao Xian Zhang*
18. Open Up to Tame Tiger	*18. Pi Shen Fu Hu*
19. Transfer Saber	*19. Jiao Dao Shih*
20. Kick with Right Heel	*20. You Deng Jiao*
21. Hit Tiger Left and Right	*21. Zuo You Da Hu Shih*
22. Kick with Right Heel	*22. You Deng Jiao*
23. Transfer Sabre and Chop Downward	*23. Jiao Dao Pi*
24. Raise Foot and Stab	*24. Di Jiao Ci*
25. Conceal Sabre to Present Palm	*25. Zang Dao Xian Zhang*
26. Turn Round and Stab	*26. Hui Shen Ci*
27. Curling Sabre Left and Right	*27. Zuo You Liao Dao*

Traditonal Yang Style Sabre Form continued..

28. Jump and Conceal Sabre
29. Step Aside to Cast Shuttle
30. Conceal Sabre to Present Palm
31. Transfer Sabre
32. Step Back to Seven Stars
33. Return to Beginning

28. *Tiao Bu Zang Dao*
29. *Yi Bu Pao Suo*
30. *Zang Dao Xian Zhang*
31. *Jiao Dao Shih*
32. *Tui Bu Qi Xing*
33. *Huan Yuan*

Right:
Grandmaster Ip demonstrates
one of the Sabre postures

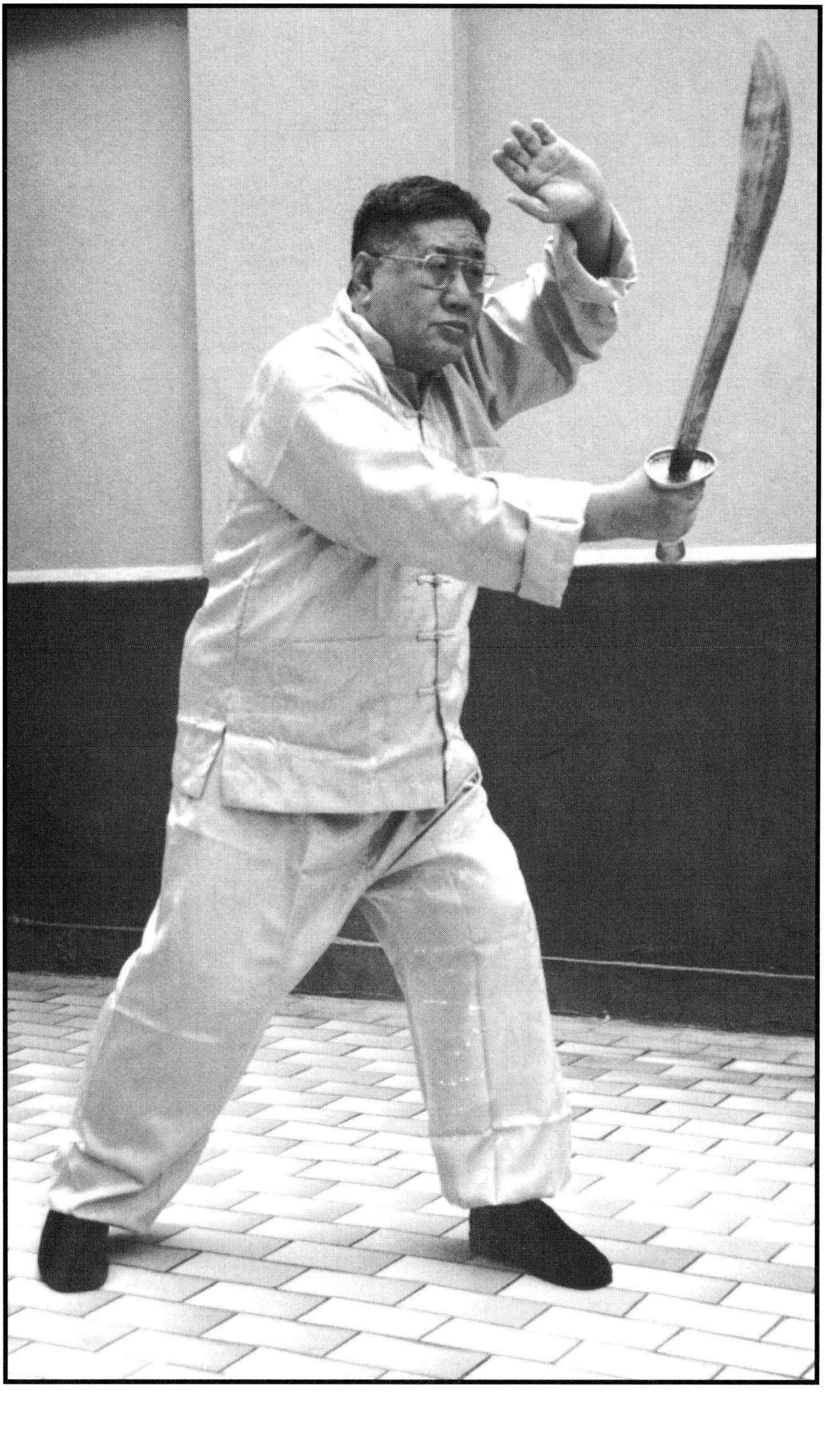

Appendix 5

Traditional Yang Style Tai Chi Spear Techniques

Thirteen Spear Techniques

First Set :

四粘槍　　　　　　　**Si Nian Qiang**

Stab to the Heart　　　*Ci Xin*
Stab to the Feet　　　 *Ci Zu*
Stab to the Shoulder　*Ci Jian*
Stab to the Throat　　*Ci Hou*

Second Set:

四散槍　　　　　　　**Si San Qiang**

Stab to the Chest　　 *Ci Xiong*
Stab to the Shoulder　*Ci Jian*
Stab to the Leg　　　 *Ci Tui*
Stab to the Face　　　*Ci Mian*

Third Set:

四櫻槍　　　　　　　**Si Ying Qiang**

Pull Down　　*Cai Qiang*
Split　　　　 *Lie Qiang*
Throw　　　　*Reng Qiang*
Slice　　　　 *Chan Qiang*

Fourth Set :

纏槍一路　　　　　　**Chan Qiang**

Entwining Spear　　　*Chan Qiang*

Appendix 6

Glossary of Chinese Terms

Glossary

An	- *Push*
An	- *Natural*
An Jin	- *Push energy*
Ba Gua	- *Eight Triagrams*
Bing	- *Illness*
Bu Diu Ding	- *Not confronting or disengaging*
Chang Chuan	- *Long Fist System of the Chinese Martial Arts*
Cai	- *Pull down*
Cai Jin	- *Pull down energy power*
Chi	- *Intrinsic energy or life force which is within all living things; also written as Qi.*
Chi	- *Ultimate (as in Tai Chi - the Chinese word "Chi" is a different word from Chi as in the internal energy)*
Choi	- *Yielding*
Chong Xin	- *Weighting*
Chuan Tze	- *A famous Chinese philosopher*
Chuan Shen Pai Lien	- *Turn body to sweep lotus*
Cuo	- *To dampen or foil*
Dan Tian	- *The field of Chi, an acupuncture point located between one and a half to two inches below the navel.*
Dao	- *Banner i.e. a long strip of flexible material displaying for example a slogan, which is supported on either side. In Tai Chi theory, the waist is referred to as a banner which is supported by the legs on either side.*
Ding	- *Being still*
Ding	- *Resist*
Diu	- *Throw*
Dong Jin	- *Understanding the essence of power*
Gan Kun Gen Xun	- *Refers to the four corners*

Appendix 6

Gu	- *Being attentive*
Gu Dang	- *Resonating drum*
Gan Jue	- *Sensitivity*
Hou	- *Fire*
Huo	- *Spry*
Laozi	- *A famous Taoist*
Jau	- *to flee (in Tai Chi theory it means, "to divert while seeming to flee")*
Ji	- *Press*
Ji Chu	- *The fundamentals*
Ji Jin	- *Press energy power*
Jie	- *To complement another person's force*
Jie Jin	- *Intercepting energy*
Jin	- *Essence of power; there are many types of Jin power due to the different applications*
Jin	- *Metal*
Jin	- *Advancing*
Kang	- *Confront*
Kan Li Zhen Dui	- *Refers to the four sides of a square*
Kao	- *Shoulder*
Kong	- *To discharge*
Kua	- *The joints between the thighs and the pelvis*
Lian	- *Link*
Lie	- *To split*
Lin	- *Linking or joining*
Ling	- *Nimble*
Liang Di	- *"measure" the opponent; here "measure" is concerned with assessing the opponent's power and ability.*
Lou Hsih Au Pu	- *Brush knee and push*
Lu	- *Roll back*
Lu Jin	- *Roll back energy power*

Man Gong Chu Xi Huo	- *Slow work produces detail and quality goods*
Mu	- *Wood*
Nian	- *Adhere*
Nian	- *Touching*
On	- *Natural*
Pan	- *Gazing*
Pao Hu Kwei Shan	- *Embrace tiger and return to mountain*
Pe Shen Chui	- *Punch and parry*
Peng	- *Ward off*
Peng Jin	- *Ward off energy power*
Pian	- *Tilt*
Qi	- *Flag*
Qing	- *Lightness*
Rou	- *To knead*
She Ji Cong Ren	- *To abandon oneself, to follow the opponent*
Shen	- *Spirit*
Shen	- *Body*
Shi	- *Substantial*
Shou Shou	- *Teaching and receiving*
Shuang Chong	- *Double weighting*
Shu	- *Extension*
Shui	- *Water*
Si Zheng Si Ou	- *The four directions and four corners*
Sui	- *Yielding*
Sui	- *Follow*
Tan Pien Hsia Shih	- *Snake creeps down*
Tai	- *Grand or great*
Teng	- *Being still*
Ting Jin	- *Listening energy*
Tou Ding Xuan	- *To suspend one's head*

Tu	- Earth
Tui	- Stepping back
Tui Shou	- Push Hands
Wen Da	- Question and answer
Wu Chi	- From nothingness or stillness
Wu Hang	- Five Elements
Wu Shu	- Chinese Martial Arts
Xian Xiang Gong	- Coil Incense Kung
Xin	- Heart, which usually refers to the "mind" in Chinese
Xing	- Expression
Xu	- Insubstantial
Xu Ling Ding Jin	- Empty the crown to push up the energy
Yao	- Waist
Yang	- Positive polarity of the grand ultimate while the negative polarity being the Yin
Yau	- To knead
Yeh Ma Fung Tsung	- Parting the horse's mane
Yi	- Intention of the mind
Yi Dou Chi Dou	- When the intent arrives, Chi will also arrive
Yi Jing Zhi Dong	- Use calmness to subdue agitation
Yi Rou Zhi Gong	- Use softness to overcome rigidity or hardness
Yi Qu Qiu Zhi	- Use spiralling motion to overcome linear force
Yin	- The negative pole of Tai Chi. Opposite of Yang
Yu Nu Chuen Shu	- Jade maiden casting shuttle
Yu Fung Shih Pi	- Apparent close up and push
Yuan	- Wholeness
Zheng	- Upright and precise
Zhou	- Elbow
Zi Ji	- To know the opportunity

Zhong	*- Centre*
Zhong Ting	*- Centred*
Zou	*- As if to flee*

Miscellaneous

& Alternative Health

An International & the UK's Leading Tai Chi Magazine

Published since 1994 by Master Ding, 6th Generation Yang Family Tai Chi Chuan and an international Tai Chi master.

Every quarterly issue features in-depth articles on all aspects of Tai Chi Chuan - history, theory, martial application as well as interviews with leading Tai Chi Masters. The magazine also features the theory and practice of Alternative Health Therapies - Shiatsu, Acupuncture, Aromatherapy and so on, rounded out by articles on Chinese philosophy, Taoism, Zen, Reviews, News and Letters.

TCAH is essential reading for those with an interest in Internal Arts, Alternative Therapies and the philosophies that shape them. Readers find it both educational and informative! Do not miss out on your copy of TCAH!

Copies can also be ordered from U.K outlets such as WH Smith, Menzies, Martins, your local newsagents or **take up a subscription NOW!!**

Web page: www.taichiwl.demon.co.uk

Subscription Offer ....

Annual (4 issues) - £12 (UK) £16 (Europe) £20 (Rest of the World)
2 Years (9 issues) - £24 (UK) £32 (Europe) £40 (Rest of the World)
However, if you are interested in a sample copy, just send £4 (incl.p&p)

Please make cheque payable to ***TCAH*** and send it to :
TCAH (BS), P.O. BOX 6404, LONDON E18 1EX, UK.
(Note: Overseas subscribers must send a bankdraft drawn from any British Bank)

For more information about the Academy,
its different international branches
and courses on offer,
do write to us at our headquarters:

**Maybank House, Unit C,
208 Maybank Road,
London E18 1ET,
United Kingdom**

or P.O.Box 6404,
London E18 1EX,
United Kingdom

or email us at :
jdiatcc@taichiwl.demon.co.uk

or visit our website:
www.taichiwl.demon.co.

Tel: +44 (20) 85502 9307 / +44 (20) 8551 7553

The John Ding International Academy of Tai Chi Chuan
established in 1992

Founder:
Master John Ding
6th Generation of
the Yang Family Lineage

Chief Instructor:
Dr. Alan Ding

JDIATCC for:
tradition, authenticity, depth and excellence

Aims:
- To preserve and promote the practice of Traditional Yang Family Tai Chi Chuan as passed down through several generations of the Yang Family.
- To promote the health and harmony of mind, body and spirit.
- To explore personal strengths and weaknesses and spiritual growth.
- To enable Tai Chi Chuan practitioners to gain better insight and understanding of the principles of Tai Chi Chuan

Courses Available:
Quality instruction available for Beginners to Advanced level in all aspects of the Traditional Yang Family Tai Chi Chuan training system.

We also welcome Tai Chi practitioners or instructors with at least 4 years experience of Yang Style Tai Chi Chuan who wish to train up as qualified instructors of the Academy.

Right:
Dr. Alan Ding demonstrating
"Snake Creeps Down"
Tai Chi Chuan posture.

205

Right:
Three Generations of Yang Family Tai Chi Chuan.
Left to right: Master Ding, Grandmaster Ip and Dr. Alan Ding

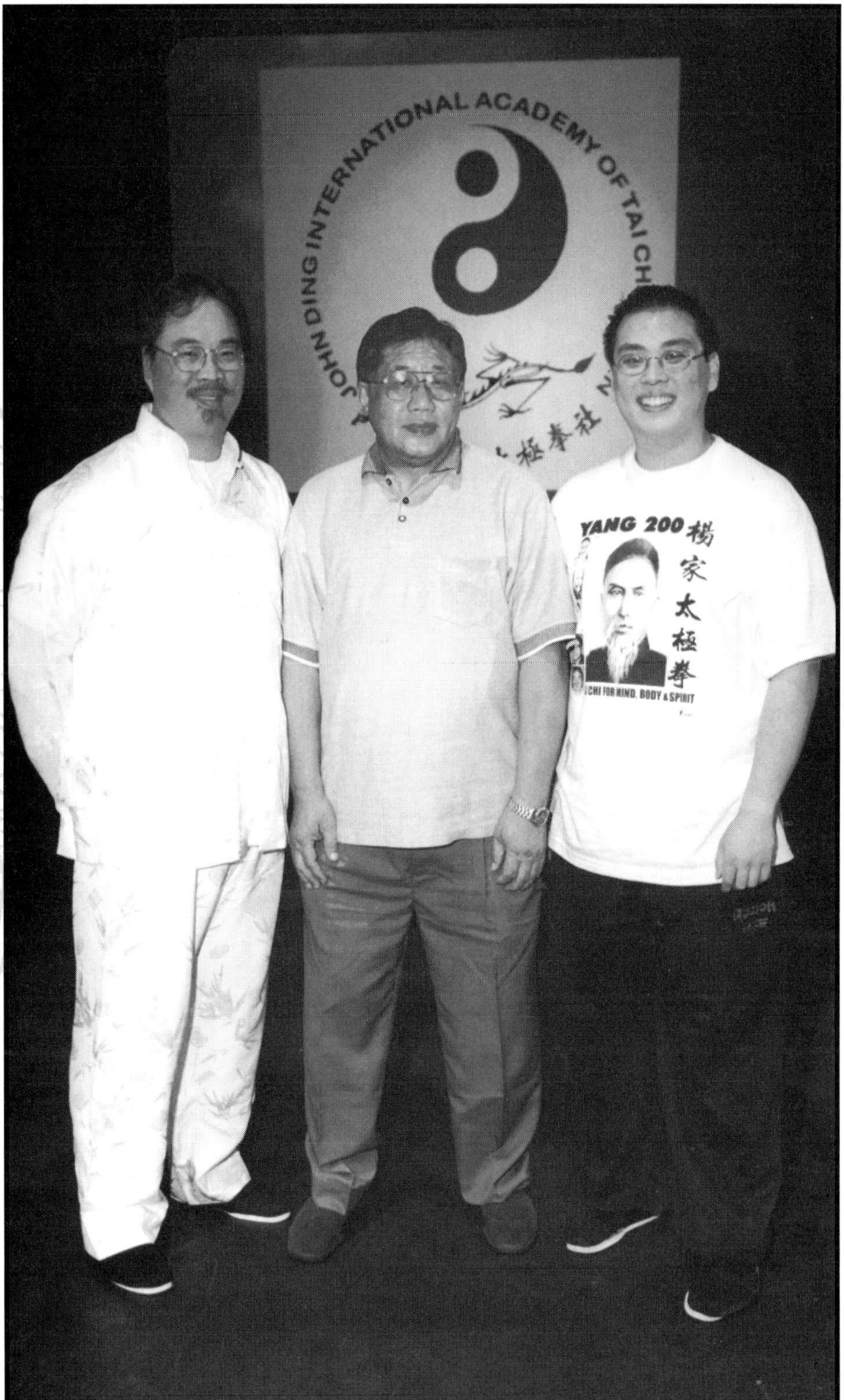
JOHN DING INTERNATIONAL ACADEMY OF TAI
YANG 200
楊家太極拳

Notes

Right:
"Golden Rooster Standing on One Leg" posture